PRAISE FOR *INSIDE OUT*

"There are numerous voices in the current conversation about the future of the church. Some of them say that we are done. Others point to our decline, and others are content with quips on social media. There are some, however, that speak boldly about the mission of Jesus and His church, and Wayne Bray is one of those voices. I would encourage you to listen to him. Specifically, I hope that you read his words. In the pages of this book, he lays out simple yet powerful ways for the church of Jesus Christ to regain the same passion that drove Jesus to lay down His life for the world. This is a strong book with a timely message written by a pastor who has lived out what he talks about."
Clayton King
Evangelist, Teaching Pastor at Newspring Church
Founder of Crossroads Summer Camps

Wayne Bray takes a poignant, convicting look at society in America and it's relationship to the church. This is a captivating read! Bray provides an effective framework that can easily help Christ-followers embrace the mission that is always on God's heart -- loving everyone with a spirit of truth and grace. While the issues in our world are complicated, the point Bray makes is clear and needed: Christians must stop pushing people away from the cross with prejudice, anger, and ignorance.
Jeremy Morton – Co-Pastor, FBC Woodstock, GA

This book, *Inside Out* "Gets It!" It's the must read book for Churches and Christians with passion to make a REAL difference in their culture.
Bill Purvis – Author of "Make a Break For It"
Lead Pastor, Cascade Hills Church, Columbus, GA

How does the church engage a chaotic culture with the gospel without losing its soul? Wayne Bray has provided a useful description of the times in which we live and some valuable prescriptions for how the church can break out of its lethargy and self-absorption and become mission-driven once again. This will be a helpful tool for every church leader for whom "the way we've always done it" isn't good enough.
Michael Duduit - *Editor of Preaching Magazine*
Dean, Clamp Divinity School of Anderson University in Anderson, SC

Wayne Bray's book, *Inside Out*, paints an accurate picture of what the world and the church have become, but the truth can get rather painful to acknowledge at times. This book will be a great help to you as you attempt to focus on the main thing, which is after all to keep the main thing the main thing.
Brian Stowe – *Senior Pastor, First Baptist Church Plant City, FL*

Inside Out, by Dr. Wayne Bray, will help you stay in love with Jesus' church and its ministry even if you are dismayed by its current civil wars (worship, generationalism, traditions, theology.) His approach to multi generational church shows us how to leave a legacy the young will appreciate at least as much as they admire.
Dick Lincoln – *Retired Pastor, Shandon Baptist Church, Columbia, SC*
Past President, South Carolina Baptist Convention

Wayne Bray is a great example of a pastor who not only wants to see the local church make a kingdom advance but provides the type of leadership God uses to make it happen. His book *Inside Out* gets to the root of the challenges that Christian leaders in North America are facing, insightfully moves the reader to reset their thinking, and gives tools and encouragement to move a congregation to minister inside out in an upside down culture. This book is well worth the time for any leader who desires to grow and to make an impact on their community.
Steve Parr - *Author of "Why They Stay"*
VP of Staff Development, Georgia Baptist Mission Board

Distraction, division and discouragement characterize the American church in a culture marked by tribalism and hostility. Two thirds of our churches are declining or dying while whole communities have no access to the gospel in a way that is culturally relevant. Dr. Wayne Bray argues forcefully that the answer is to turn the church "inside out" by dying to self and equipping our people for missionary living. This book is a clarion call to action, unity and new life for the local church.

Al Phillips – *Director of Missions, Greenville Baptist Association (Greenville, SC)*

It's been my joy to watch God use Wayne Bray as a small town pastor in Millen, GA and now as the leader of a forward thinking multi-site movement in South Carolina. And to know that where it matters, he's basically the same person.

Bobby Braswell – *Associational Missions Strategist, Middle Baptist Association (Sylvania, GA)*

INSIDE OUT

Christian Hope in a World of Contradictions

*The only hope for a world turned upside down
is a church turned inside out*

WAYNE BRAY

INSIDE OUT

Christian Hope in a World of Contradictions

©2019 by Wayne Bray
All rights reserved.

Published by Rainer Publishing
www.RainerPublishing.com
Spring Hill, TN

ISBN: 978-1-948022-14-9
Printed in the United States of America

Scripture quotations are from The Holy Bible, English Standard Version® (ESV®), copyright © 2001 by Crossway, a publishing ministry of Good News Publishers. Used by permission. All rights reserved.

CONTENTS

Part One - The World Turned Upside-down 15
   Organized Anarchy 17
   Narcissistic Utilitarianism 25
   American Nightmares 33
   Jenga Nation 43
   8-Tracks and iPhones 53

Part Two - The Church Turned Inside-Out 61
   Drop the Rocks 63
   Trade Suits for Boots 77
   Pull Back the Curtain 89
   Surrender Self 101
   Awaken to Purpose 113

FOREWORD

A well-worn quote says, "everybody complains about the weather but nobody does anything about it." It might be said today that there is a lot of complaining about the moral and spiritual erosion of our society but there seems to be little movement in terms of doing something about it. One might ask, "whose job is it to keep a finger on the pulse of culture and correct it when gone astray?" Some would say it can be done through legislation and politics. Others believe more education will do the trick. Still others advocate that there are no moral absolutes so "leave me alone and don't try to impose your morals on me!" It is that kind of thinking that has led our world to being turned upside down over the past several decades. The real answer to the "whose job is it" question is the Church of the resurrected Jesus!

It takes only a brief glance at the daily news to see that our country is in trouble. Sadly, statistics and reports reveal that churches in America are also in trouble. It is one thing to measure church attendance and the size of budgets. It is another to ask "is there any cultural and community transformation taking place through the ministry of local churches?" Here at the South Carolina Baptist Convention, that question is most often answered by simply asking, "which way is your arrow pointing?" If the arrow is pointed inward, that is a sure indicator that the bulk of the activity of the church is for the members only. If it is pointing outward, that is usually a good sign that they are seeking to engage the community with the Gospel.

Wayne Bray is a pastor/practitioner who shares keen insight in helping churches turn their arrow from pointing inside to out.

While the first half of the book accurately explains some of the ways our world has been turned upside down in recent years, the second half provides both challenge and encouragement to pastors and leaders that EVERY church can turn their arrow around. At times it is descriptive and much like a visit to the doctor, it might hurt a little. At other times it is prescriptive and it is there you will find help, and even perhaps a cure, leading to a more healthy approach to church life.

It is a rare occasion to meet a pastor or church leader who intentionally seeks to lead a church to be inward in focus. More times than not it occurs slowly and happens because of unrealistic expectations placed on the pastor to meet selfish demands and accommodate personal preferences. *Inside Out* addresses the sinfulness of such attitudes and provides biblical and practical advice on how to overcome these challenges which can lead to a church being turned inside out. For sure, these changes can only take place by the Spirit of God and must be preceded by prayer, fasting and sound biblical leadership.

Because our world has been so dramatically turned upside down in the past many years, the urgency of the hour does not allow the church the luxury of doing business as usual. Wayne's words are prophetic, practical and personal so do not read *Inside Out* if you wish a comfortable, leisure read. If, however, you have a stirring in your soul that all is not right in the world and a conviction that Jesus is the answer, then by all means read it with an open Bible, a prayerful attitude and a willing spirit to be personally turned inside out in order to reach a world turned upside down.

Gary Hollingsworth
Executive Director / Treasurer
South Carolina Baptist Convention

INTRODUCTION

The opening sentence of the Charles Dickens' classic, A *Tale of Two Cities*, puts our current culture in proper perspective. "It was the best of times. It was the worst of times."[1] This could have been written of the United States in the 21st Century. America has been blessed to enjoy both a prolonged economic prosperity and dependable national security. Yes, these are the best of times in many ways, yet I fear it may be the worst of times in many others. We are facing some serious challenges that can't be solved by financial strength or military might. No matter how our jobs report or economic forecast might look, America is headed towards a spiritual great depression.

This might seem to be an unavoidable result of the world's rejection of gospel truth, but it's not that simple. While the world has been turned upside down, the church has simultaneously turned inward, losing its influence in a crowd of competing voices. We still believe that Jesus is the answer to the world's problems, yet no one seems to be asking our opinion anymore. Instead of bringing the world to Christ, the church has often produced more confusion than conversion. The American people are more divided than ever, debating issues like social justice, religious liberty, right to life/choice, racial discrimination, immigration, education reform, gun control, economic disparity, gender inequality, sexual orientation and countless more. No two people, including Christians, seem to agree completely on all of these issues. It's enough to make your head spin.

While America once appreciated a predictable set of unquestioned principles, a major social shift has taken place, exposing the fault lines in our moral foundation. This change has empowered unconventional ideologies, while making the radical more routine. We're still called the United States of America, but our nation grows more divided every day. From a football player's protest of racial injustice in San Francisco, California - to a Colorado business owner's refusal to bake a cake because of his religious convictions - to a violent rally of racists in Charlottesville, Virginia, Americans are a divided people. Erratic behavior has become the norm in American life, but the Christian's response to this chaos has been as unpredictable as the events themselves.

Why do we need this book?

Having been born and raised the son of a Southern Baptist pastor, and having now served as a pastor myself for over 20 years, I've witnessed the good and the bad of the Christian Church in North America. The constant cultural chaos rages outside the walls of our churches, yet Christians are distracted by peripheral matters and seem to be disinterested in the tragic trend that surrounds them. While we believe the gospel is the ultimate solution to the world's problem of spiritual darkness, followers of Jesus are too busy fighting each other to shine the light.

We can divide this book into two simple sections: Upside Down and Inside Out. I will use the first half of the book (Chapters 1-5) to explain how the world has turned upside down, while the second half of the book (Chapters 6-10) will offer a practical hope for tomorrow, a church turned inside out. These are a collection of my observations and convictions related to some serious problems we are currently facing in our nation. I hope you'll embrace my sincere desire to move the church toward missional action in order to engage the culture for the glory of God.

The content of the first five chapters is admittedly weighty, including subjects like ethics, philosophy, sociology, and American Christianity. My hope is to reveal some of the cultural context that has led to our current chaos. We have seen liberty taken to an extreme, producing a form of anarchy where authority is deemed the enemy and every man his own god. Our self-centered culture has taught us to push for prosperity at any cost, while ignoring the fault lines in our moral foundations. The future of our nation, therefore, remains uncertain, and the legacy of American Christianity as unsure as weather in springtime.

We must change the trend and restore hope for the next generation of believers. Chapters 6-10 will explore some significant steps Christians must take in order to make a significant impact in the days ahead. I believe the only hope for a world turned upside down is a church turned inside out. It is my goal to help Christians and churches discover how they can begin that process. We've all seen first hand how Christians can manage to make the gospel appear unattractive to a lost world. It's like we have the antidote to humanity's poison, but no one knows how to administer the cure effectively. While this book will not be an exhaustive list of problems or solutions, it is a good place to start.

Wake Up Call

This upside down world seems to be enjoying a ride down a violent river, but it's quickly approaching some dangerous rapids. Everyone is busy arguing over the seats, while the boat floats ever closer to the falls. Where does the Christian church fit in all this chaos? We are right in the middle of the mud slinging and mayhem. Distracted by our politics and populism, drawn away by greed and pride, Christians are as divided as any other group in America. Everyone appears to be writing his own rulebook as the boat approaches its inevitable end.

Sadly, the average Christian stands silent on the banks of the muddy river of public opinion and political correctness. We've constructed beautiful buildings on the land and posted signs declaring everyone is welcome in the dry comfort of our churches. All the while, men, women, boys, and girls are drowning as they float by our buildings. Church leaders discuss the sad state of affairs, and

Christians pray continually that God will save those who are hopelessly passing us in the water. Yet our hands stay clean as we wave, and no mud is on our Sunday shoes.

What is wrong with us? Do Christians even care about the lost anymore? While many retreat into isolation, we are called turn the church inside out and awaken to the mission to which we've been called. Believers must wade into the muddy waters to rescue the perishing. They are calling for help, gasping for air, and reaching for a hand. There we stand on the banks, our hands filled with less important things. Christians must lay down our debates and distractions in order to jump into the river. Are you ready and willing to dive in?

PART ONE

THE WORLD TURNED UPSIDE-DOWN

CHAPTER ONE

ORGANIZED ANARCHY

The Twilight Zone

Cultural contradictions abound on every side as we hurriedly progress ever closer to the hypocritical social ideal of selective tolerance for some. Every American seems to be in favor of racial equality, economic equity, religious freedom, and social justice as long as they are allowed to define the terms. Surprisingly, the definitions of freedom, equality, and even morality have been altered while we were American dreaming. It's like we're watching a bad episode of the Twilight Zone that never ends. While a consensus morality had been assumed in the past, we have been awakened to a nation where every man determines his own standard of right and wrong. Moral anarchy abounds.

Authoritative structures that have been in place for decades are now being questioned at every turn, and any established systems are being challenged from an extremely biased viewpoint. From established political parties to company loyalty, skepticism and distrust are now found in the place of confidence and allegiance. Previous social norms are now considered outdated by many who assume that any standard conceived by a different generation, under different circumstances, must be called into question. This new age of postmodern thought considers it their full right to reinvent these "archaic" social standards.[2]

Perhaps the most obvious recent example of this is the debate over gender identity. This issue reveals an inconsistent logic in our society. For example, one might errantly argue that science renders the belief in a Creator irrational, while holding to a dogmatic defense of gender neutrality that ignores biological evidence that clearly contradicts their position. Why? Everyone picks and chooses his/her facts these days. It's become standard practice for a man to begin with a conclusion and choose or reject evidence based on its support of his claim.

Generally speaking, the new assumption is, "if it has been…it should no longer be." No one seems to trust the old rules anymore. Every authority is now being called into question, and some powers certainly need to be dethroned because of their intolerable corruption. The "Me Too Movement" has revealed how a terrible social injustice, like the abuse of women, can easily become an accepted norm. Still, we appear to be in the middle of a major overcorrection where every institution, hierarchy, and authority now finds itself under a microscope of biased inspection. While accountability and transparency are imperative, objectivity and civility are equally important. "With a loss of 'cultural authority' especially in the United States, almost everything seems weightless and up for grabs. As the saying goes: 'We know the price of everything and the value of nothing.'"[3]

My wife has experienced this first hand in education. She has taught elementary school for over a decade, three different grades in two different states. There have been some positive changes in education during this time, but there have also been some disturbing trends. One such negative change is the perceived decline in parental respect and support for teachers. Like many of you, I was raised to see disrespect of a teacher, or any authority for that matter, as equivalent to disrespecting my own parents. This was prominent reasoning just a few decades ago, but is now a rare opinion.

I will admit that my wife and I have been tempted to play the blame game ourselves through the years. I remember one morning I was called to the school by my son's kindergarten teacher. She reached out to me because he had been acting up in class. After leaving work and driving to his school, I went to the door and ask to speak with my son (not the teacher). My son and I had a serious "conversation" about behavior in the middle of the hallway. All I needed to know is that he had disrespected his teacher. The details of the story were not as important as the headline. My son had been disrespectful.

Something has happened in our society over the past few decades that changed the way parents think. We're not short on experts who might offer suggestions as to the cause of this phenomenon, but regardless of the cause...this is our new reality. It is now the norm for parents to begin the conversation from a defensive posture, assuming the best of their children in every case. These parents don't affirm a teacher's authority. Instead, they indirectly teach their children to become fools by undermining the authority of those who have given their lives to serve them as educators. When parents choose to defend a guilty child without cause, the child is left without a standard of discipline to go by.

Education is only one of many examples of how our society has embraced an organized anarchy. Authority has now been redefined as an enemy to criticize rather than an influence to admire. Another clear example of this trend is the reputation of law enforcement. I was raised to honor and respect police officers, to assume the best in them and pray for their safety. We always saw the police as servants of the community, willing to place themselves in harm's way to protect us. When dad taught me to drive, he made sure I understood the protocol, should I be pulled over. I was to do everything the policeman said, not because he was a man of character, but because he was in a position of authority.

First, let's acknowledge that, like any profession, some policemen are not "good cops." Many Americans understandably fear law enforcement because of discrimination and corruption. This sort of distorted evil is unacceptable and must be acknowledged and rebuked by Christians when brought to light in our society. However, this fear should only be present in a few extreme cases in our nation. While there are countless law enforcement officers in the United States, only a fraction of them are guilty of using excessive force. These few unacceptable cases of abuse, however, have caused a ripple effect across the nation. Some reporters seem to sit waiting for any opportunity to report police brutality, while no one reports the countless contributions these men and women in uniform provide every day. Some have taken the actions of a few guilty officers and passed judgment on the entire profession.

Today, everyone pushes back against the rules, against any authority, and against any established standard, assuming the worst of them all. And in the absence of a universal standard, everyone writes his own rulebook. Everyone defines the terms in his own way, from his own perspective, to fit his own circumstances. This philosophical shift brings to mind Bill Clinton's infamous parsing of the definition of the word "is" during the Monica Lewinski scandal. Of course, everyone saw his comments as deceitful at the time, but our culture has since embraced his approach and applied Clinton's philosophy to their personal lives. Everyone writes his own rules and claims to be his own god. How can this be true? Have Americans fooled themselves? Have we bought into a bankrupt moral account? The answer is simple, YES!

This Neo-American ideology is intoxicating to millions of citizens. The general public is drunk with the new wine of an elusive tyrannical tolerance where the standards are always two for one. While the culture remains fluent in the language of liberty, the moral absolutes assumed non-negotiable just a few years ago now have a large neon asterisk beside them. The small print has changed, and a new era of contradiction and hypocrisy has been ushered in.

A Long-expected Surprise

Henry David Thoreau had it right when he said, "Rather than love, than money, than fame, give me truth."[4] Our journey must begin with truth regardless of the intended destination, but few people would agree with this conviction today. Instead, truth is seen as a subjective cushion, a travel pillow to be repositioned to make us more comfortable as we journey through life. Truth, however, is not a cushion but a rock, absolute, consistent, and surpassing the limitations of circumstance and time. Postmodern

Americans, however, have moved away from this consistent rock, trading it for the individualized flexibility of personalized reality. "They...embrace realism concerning truth and knowledge, and most deny that anything can be known with certainty. Each culture creates its own truth."[5] The individual battles we see on political and social issues are merely evidence of a more foundational war against objective truth.

You've likely heard the old proverb, often attributed to Mark Twain, "Never let the truth get in the way of a good story." Americans have adopted this approach to many areas of their lives. They no longer allow the truth, reality, or logic to interfere with their preconceived ideas. And so, they choose to stand their ground on the quicksand of intentional ignorance instead of the firm foundation of knowable truth. Discourse is dead in America, and no one even went to the funeral. The idea of taking all points into consideration before making a decision is a foreign concept these days. Ironically, the same people who are immovable on certain issues, trade in their convictions on others, choosing to buy in completely to the unsubstantiated opinions of others for the sake of political leverage.

Entire philosophical beliefs, moral positions, even major political campaigns are based on the hopes that people will take the speaker at his word and not fact-check the details. People love speaking in vague generalizations, and many intentionally make unfounded statements without any accountability for their actions, simply because they know the benefit of speculation and confusion will far outweigh any question of their character for making such an unfounded claim. When a standard is unpopular, people attempt to discount that standard in order to legitimize their own desires. It seems everyone approaches any discussion with a predetermined opinion that is above debate or dialogue. What is true? No one seems to care.

This new "abnormal normal" should not come as a surprise to any of us. Our loss of a standard is a direct result of human hypocrisy, which has led the American people to embrace subjective false assumptions rather than objective absolutes. It's easy for well-meaning people to jump to conclusions and adopt views on a variety of issues before being completely informed. In fact, it's now common for people to reject the facts simply because they're afraid it might contradict or confuse their own preferred position. This is a crisis of conviction, but it's not just "those people." Christians are just as guilty as anyone else.

The world is turned upside down, but we saw it coming a mile away. Christians have anticipated the arrival of this postmodern dominance for decades. It's like we've been eating Big Macs and tater tots every meal for decades, and now we're surprised our health has declined and we're overweight. Why does everyone seem so shocked to see our society in the ICU? I once heard Andy Stanley say, "Our direction, not our intention, will determine our destination."[6] While this is an elementary idea, our nation doesn't seem to get it. Some seem to think they can choose any path they desire but maintain the right to choose an unrelated destination in the end. The American people intentionally made a choice to walk a particular direction decades ago, and that path has led to this destination.

Christians saw the road signs along the way, warning of the impending threat. This destination has been on our GPS for years, and we all knew it was coming. We've heard the occasional voice, "recalculating...recalculating" - instructing us to "make a U-turn ahead," but we just kept driving as if we didn't hear a thing. This new age of thinking has led to an obvious "breakdown of social and religious consensus," which has produced extreme social chaos.[7] But the confusion is not limited to the outsiders. As the church has turned inward, the conflict has become stronger and the rhetoric louder.

America's biggest problem is not the economy or the political shenanigans of each election cycle. The truth is that we don't know where we're going anymore. America's moral map is complex and confusing, and our compass has been broken for decades. God is certainly willing to direct the paths of anyone who trusts and acknowledges Him (Proverbs 3:5-6), but Christians appear as lost as unbelievers these days, too busy fighting each other to rescue the perishing. As a result, we've been walking aimlessly through a major social transition, attempting to maintain our character but unwilling to admit we've lost our soul. Many Americans claim that we don't need a moral map at all, arguing we've outgrown such archaic restrictions. They question if one single map can really be trusted to provide directions for every traveler. So, every man creates his own custom coordinates, drawn exclusively by his own personal preferences and desires. Reality? Who cares? Modern man considers himself to have risen above the need for a divine guidance. And so we stay the course. The GPS has now been set. Our destination is destruction, and our nation has fallen asleep at the wheel.

Extremism and The Mainstream Minority

Any honest Christian would have to admit that he's been guilty of hypocrisy on occasion, wrongly adopting a circumstantial approach to ethics and morality rather than holding himself to the same standard he applies to others. Moral inconsistencies abound. Every side has an extreme group of vocal activists who are determined to change the opinion of everyone else in the nation on any number of disputes. The issues may vary from person to person, but the strategy and obsession is common to them all. Winning the argument tends to be much preferred to actually doing the right thing. Our desire to BE right seems to be much stronger than the desire to DO right.

Instead of approaching controversial social issues with common sense, people tend to choose a side first and then ask what the question is. While everyone cries political compromise, hyperpartisanship rules the day in America.[8] The mainstream has dried up, and the foundations of the political establishment have been exposed. In the absence of reason and discourse, extremism has become commonplace.[9] Both sides of every issue have adopted a militant approach to virtually every moral dilemma we face as a nation, and the media enjoys adding fuel to the fire. The idea of an unbiased media seems to be a foreign concept in our nation, as news outlets have adopted an entertainment mentality in their reporting strategy.[10]

In the absence of a standard, we have a bunch of grown men and women fighting like children on the playground of popular opinion. Choose any channel, and you'll find the selected "experts" who are prepared to attack at first opportunity. Ironically, these moral militants from both sides fight in the name of freedom and justice, and they seem to be defending the very same freedoms from opposite perspectives. The American people actually possess a common dream, but this dream is being destroyed by our own ignorance of truth and hunger for power.

And so it continues; the politicians and pundits parade around in the waiting room while our nation remains in the ICU of history. The parade is loud, and everyone appears to be enjoying the show. All the while, our nation is on life support, clinging to the hope of every breath. After the spectacle has ended and the crowds chant no more, all that remains is the truth, reality, and the heart of the American people. But what is the truth? Sadly, we are a nation in moral chaos, caused by the same poison contained in the forbidden fruit thousands of years ago, sin.

The American dream has been terribly perverted, and our individual rights have been translated into personal entitlements motivated by pride, greed, and an insatiable lust for more. This undying thirst cannot be quenched by political policies, and no perfumed moral agenda can overwhelm the stench of our tainted motive. We, the American people, have now become our own worst enemies, and this dueling extremism has spilt over into the Christian church. Like a spiritual standoff, compromise wars against condemnation. Neither is the answer to the world's problems, but both serve as spiritual barriers to the mission of the church. So the world remains disoriented, unable to make sense of life.

It's every man for himself, as a multitude of people look out for a different number one. Anarchy rules the day as the trickling mainstream rolls down the slippery slope of morality. The world truly has turned upside down, and nothing seems to make sense anymore. It's hard for Christians to see any hope for the future, but perhaps they are the hope the world is looking for.

CHAPTER TWO

NARCISSISTIC UTILITARIANISM

Yes, the world has turned upside down, and it's every man for himself, as anarchy rules the day. Surrounded by this confusion, most people wander aimlessly through life consumed by their own agendas, unconsciously lost in a sea of selfishness amid a superficial search for fairness for all. Attempting to chase out the darkness in the world, they find their own shadows in the end. Soon confronted by the truth of their own empty pursuit of "me", men veil their vanity in benevolence and goodwill. In one hand they hold the tools to build a bridge of compassion, in the other hand a smartphone taking a selfie for their profile pic. It's all for one, and that one is always me.

As confusing as it may be, the second cause of cultural confusion is a self-defeating logic we will refer to as Narcissistic Utilitarianism. Webster's Dictionary defines a narcissist as, "an extremely self-centered person who has an exaggerated sense of self-importance." Utilitarianism, on the other hand, is the philosophy that promotes "the greatest happiness of the greatest number of persons."[11] Neither narcissism nor utilitarianism is a new way of thinking, but they have both influenced 21st Century American society more than we can imagine.

A utilitarian ethic is a worldview that approaches every challenging moral situation with the same question. Which course of action will produce the greatest benefit for the most people? While in theory this method is logical and appears to be filled with compassion, it brings great risk because of the temptation to adjust the standard based on the circumstances. We may firmly hold to absolute truth and believe that our circumstance should always yield to the standard of right and wrong, but consistency in convictions is more difficult when the threat of loss is personal. Circumstantial ethics is so prevalent in our day, and like it or not we are all attracted to it. This renders an individual's definition of right and wrong subject to the circumstances that surround him. This explains a lot in regard to our culture's love affair with itself, where people do whatever makes them feel better.

People want to focus on the personal benefit of their decisions without being confronted by the negative impact those decisions might have on other people. They live in a fantasyland of selfish denial, while promoting a benevolent agenda as a guise. "Someone could have a grand fantasy life, but reality just doesn't allow those fantasies to actually occur in, well, reality."[12] If we think about the logic of a utilitarian ethic we can see that it's self-conflicting in many ways. The tension lies in one's pleasure and happiness being the goals of his life. Someone is always required to pay a price, to sacrifice someone's pleasure. He will either require this price of someone else or willingly yield his own happiness in order for the majority to become truly successful in their search of the same.

What's best for the Most People – Especially Me?

Utilitarianism is attractive at first glance because it seems to be so conscious of the needs of others, and much of our American lifestyle and logic is founded on this philosophy. Many argue that Jesus Himself promoted a utilitarian view of morality in His teachings and actions. "The utilitarian morality does recognize in human beings the power of sacrificing their own greatest good for the good of others."[13] No one can argue with the claim that Jesus taught us to willingly embrace suffering ourselves for the joy of others. He challenged His followers to love their neighbor as themselves (Luke 10:27). Consider His words leading up to the cross. "Greater love has no one than this, that someone lay down his life for his friends" (John 15:13). This is an easy verse to quote, but living it out is a different story.

"Ain't no right way, to do the wrong thing." Maybe we like it when Toby Keith sings it, but circumstances often change our tune. The confusion begins, not necessarily in the foundational statement of the principle of utilitarianism, but in its application to individual ethical dilemmas. While there are likely many others, I see two major ways utilitarianism has brought confusion to our society: the subjective views of value and justice. We can all conceive scenarios in which an action would benefit the majority of the population, but would not be a just act. Just because something is "good" for a group of people doesn't make it a "good" thing to do.[14] Let's look at the specific question of life's value. At what point has a sick man or woman's quality of life declined to the point of no longer producing enough happiness to claim an appropriate amount of value?

If the avoidance of pain is the measure by which we determine human value, we are all in trouble. Pain is an unavoidable part of life. Utilitarianism also argues that the happiness of others is produced by the usefulness of a person. Usefulness, therefore, determines value, and likewise uselessness communicates a lack of value. In such a case, where an individual is no longer useful, he/she may be found "justifiably" disposable because of his lack of happiness or his increase of pain. While these moral extremes seemed unthinkable sitting in a college ethics class just a few years ago, they're now headline news.

The lines get blurred if happiness is our only goal in life, and not just one individual's happiness...but the general happiness of the larger majority.[15] Who really holds the right to determine the definition of happiness? What makes one person happy may not bring the same level of pleasure to another. This is a subjective venture to say the least. Even more troubling is the assumption of many that the larger community possesses the right to decide for any person or people that their deficiency in happiness and pleasure constitutes a legitimate argument for the sacrifice of their life for the potential increase in happiness of the larger group. So, as crazy as this sounds...a true utilitarian community reserves the right to sacrifice the minority for the benefit of the majority. This was a foundational argument for slavery in America when the value of a slave's life was determined by his utility to his master. While we would easily reject this idea as justifying slavery, many still hold to this same thought in other areas.

Our nation is a melting pot of cultures and philosophies. This diversity of ideas, though beneficial in some ways, has often led us to combine two otherwise completely incompatible ideas to create a new conflicting concept. The United States has become a nation of benevolent narcissists. While utilitarianism preaches "the greater good," the tendency of man is to prefer the end that benefits him the most.[16] We see this in the political result of utilitarianism, which is communism. This political concept prominent in the 20th Century offers promises of communal equality while in practice fills the pockets of those in authority. Sadly, many people in America promote a headline, seeking what's best for the most people…but the small print reads, "ESPECIALLY ME!"

We've become a country that attempts to balance utilitarian practices and narcissistic motivations. The American people are conditioned to do good things in order to feel better about themselves. We don't mind giving their time and money to a good cause, as long as we receive an appropriate amount of credit for our contributions. A narcissist views other people as tools to manipulate in order to make himself feel and look better. Consider the background of the term "narcissist," and how it sounds like the common man in our day. The idea is drawn from the Greek myth of a man who is looking for love. This young man, named Narcissus, is offered the affection of a beautiful woman, but in the end he chooses to love himself instead of her. "The myth of Narcissus captures the tragedy of self-admiration, because Narcissus becomes frozen by his self-admiration and unable to connect with anyone outside himself."[17]

Most Americans are so concerned about themselves, so in love with themselves, so devoted to themselves, that they are numb to the needs of others. They scream for equal rights for all, but they whisper a much different message. "What's in it for me?" One of the biggest reasons for our moral uncertainty is the seemingly universal embrace of conditional morality and circumstantial ethics. No one likes to speak in terms of "black and white." Grey is the shade of the day. Examples of this logic abound in our modern society. From embryonic stem cell research to the forced redistribution of wealth through taxation, our nation has bought into a utilitarian ethic hook, line, and sinker. This concept ultimately promotes the "greater good," making every decision through the lens of the benefit of the majority. We all embrace this idea at some level.

A Diet Coke Erases the Fat

It seems like I've been on a diet my entire life. Weight has been an issue for me since childhood. I can remember my mom bringing home blue jeans from the department store that fit great in the waist, but the length of the legs was always too long. My pants always needed hemming because of my stocky build. It was not until I entered middle school that I realized that "Husky" wasn't a name brand of blue jeans. I would often brag about my husky jeans, little did I know what that actually meant. Imagine my disappointment to learn "husky" was a size category, NOT COOL.

Some people struggle with metabolism issues, but I've just always really liked food – like a lot. My weight has always been an issue because I've lacked the discipline required to eat a proper diet and exercise regularly. There is really no excuse; I just choose to be inconsistent. For example, I order a Big Mac and fries, but then I make it all right in my mind by ordering a Diet Coke – like this soda will magically melt away the fat grams. Needless to say, it doesn't work. I also enjoy a good salad from time to time, but I've learned that not all salads are created fat free. What goes on the salad is much more important than the salad itself.

The American people promote the greater good for all - like we order a healthy salad, but those same people can't help but throw some bacon and croutons on top. We've conditioned ourselves to demand the greater good for all, but we are compelled to order a side of entitlement. You can see it in the pick up line at your local middle school, or the check out line at Wal-Mart. When given the opportunity to place others before themselves, most people choose to stay in front. We want to be considered selfless people who care about others more than ourselves, but we'd really rather start the process tomorrow.

We want to eat our pizza and call it a diet. Ironically, hypocrisy can't hide its face forever. While true advocates of a utilitarian worldview believe the loss of one for the gain of two validates the costs, a growing number of Americans are manipulating the rules by naming themselves as the few beneficiaries at the cost of the sacrifices of many others. They can't see the reality of their true form for the fictitious reflection they've painted in the mirror.

Though sincere concern and care for others has traditionally made our nation great, a new day has dawned in America. While the message of social justice and compassion remains in the mouths of many, talk is cheap. Still hope remains. While cultural inconsistency is the new norm, these current obstacles can be seen as missional opportunities for God's people to stand out amid the backdrop of a self-centered society consumed by the unconscious drunkenness of fraudulent fidelity.

A Narcissistic Church

Sadly, this narcissistic epidemic has crossed over into the Christian Church. Most Christ followers live as if they think their opinion is the only one that matters and everyone else owes them something. "This is the ME show, and everyone else is invited to attend." They may be ready and willing to volunteer to serve other people, as long as they get the credit they deserve.[18] Self-righteous selfishness abounds in the church today. Circumstantial morality is prevalent, and the biggest problem is that believers are blind to it. Even our charity is often laced with impure motives of self-gratification and self-promotion.

It's no wonder the nation is confused. Christians are just as likely to espouse a self-serving mindset as unbelievers. I remember one occasion in my childhood when my dad (who was a pastor) was raising money to pay for a new building. It's never easy asking people to give money, but it's even more difficult when people are not promised anything in return. Somewhere along the way my dad picked up the idea to sell bricks and provide a plaque in the lobby with everyone's names that contributed. Others were given the opportunity to purchase a window and a door in memory or in honor of someone. In return, they would have the family name engraved for all to see. I'm not trying to make anyone feel guilty for such a gift, but my point is simple. People are much more likely to sacrifice their "greater good" when they can see the indirect benefit of being credited with the public display of selflessness.

It seems that most Christians have developed an unbiblical – ungodly expectation of everything in life. The call to follow Christ leads the believer to a cross not a couch. We have not been promised comfort in this journey. Such a mindset proves the error of our flawed logic. Paul attempts to teach us to live in constant acknowledgement of the worth of the cross of Christ. "Far be it from me to boast except in the cross of our Lord Jesus Christ, by which the world has been crucified to me, and I to the world" (Galatians 6:14). Later in verse 17, Paul explains that he bore the marks of Jesus. These marks were likely scars from being beaten and stoned by his persecutors.

It's a tragedy that the early church was founded on an unwavering faith that stood amid unthinkable opposition, but modern Christians can't seem to endure the discomfort of an imbalanced thermostat on Sunday morning. Perhaps the cushion in their pew is too thin, or the music a bit too loud. Everyone seems one disagreement away from shopping for a new church home. Christians today can't imagine a call to purposeful sacrifice because we've bought into a religion built on preferential satisfaction.

CHAPTER THREE

AMERICAN NIGHTMARES

The American dream has always been a goal to reach for, a vision worth defending, and a hope worthy of one's life. Millions have left their homeland to pursue this dream - this hope for more - this search for something better. While this dream was not inherently bad, Americans lost sight of the purpose of it all somewhere along the way. We bought into the narcissistic independence that named us king of our own lives, and our dream became a nightmare while we were sleeping. The search for prosperity went to everyone's head, leading the country down a path of fatal materialistic attraction and greed unlike anything we could have ever imagined. We were encouraged to dream big, but reality didn't measure up to the expectations of many.

Eventually it wasn't enough to have enough; everyone wanted more – not just more than they had...but more than anyone else had. People have always compared themselves to others, but envy and greed increased with every passing day. This eventually led to a constant state of disappointment and discontentment. Listen to the words of Solomon in Ecclesiastes 1:8, "All things are full of weariness; a man cannot utter it; the eye is not satisfied with seeing, nor the ear filled with hearing." These words describe a progression of covetousness, not simply a momentary decision, but an unfolding of desire.

The level of our dissatisfaction is so discouraging that Solomon can't even begin to describe it; the disappointment that comes with materialism "cannot be uttered." This world cannot completely satisfy us, and we can't begin to find true contentment in earthly possessions, but it sure does seem like ungodly people find happiness. They become more successful and prosperous with every passing day, but they don't seem miserable at all. Psalm 37:1-7 offers this encouragement for believers, "1 Fret not yourself because of evildoers; be not envious of wrongdoers! 2 For they will soon fade like the grass and wither like the green herb. 3 Trust in the LORD, and do good; dwell in the land and befriend faithfulness. 4 Delight yourself in the LORD, and he will give you the desires of your heart. 5 Commit your way to the LORD; trust in him, and he will act. 6 He will bring forth your righteousness as the light, and your justice as the noonday. 7 Be still before the LORD and wait patiently for Him; fret not yourself over the one who prospers in his way, over the man who carries out evil devices!"

So, the message everyone needs is the one no one wants to hear. "Wait patiently for Him." But it's not fair; I didn't get as much as he did! "Wait patiently for Him." You don't understand! I have invested all this work, time, and energy - and I have sacrificed so much for the cause. And they have done nothing! This is not right! "Wait patiently for Him; *do not fret...*" God is saying, "I've got this. Trust me." This is, in the end, what it boils down to; we must learn to trust in the Lord, even when everything around us seems to be falling apart. We must make the intentional decision to stop trying to figure everything out. Sometimes, it's just not going to make sense. This world is so messed up that logic and reasoning don't always apply to our circumstances. Ironically, it is when we learn to trust our dreams to God and wait on His timing that our confusing crooked path is made straight by his grace (Proverbs 3:5-6).

Our Golden Calf

Like us, the people of Israel were often impatient. Exodus 32 is one of many examples of their consistent inconsistency. Moses went to the mountain to meet with God, but he was taking too long to come back down. While he was gone, the people approached Aaron and demanded that he make them a god to go before them.

So Aaron collected jewelry, and made them a golden idol in the shape of a calf. Obviously Moses wasn't happy when he returned, and neither was God. How could these people who claimed to love God so foolishly reject Him? Well, our nation has fallen into the same selfish trap. We have been drawn away, distracted by the short-term attraction of momentary material gain in exchange for the long-term burden of debt and brokenness. The price we've paid to realize our dreams has been found far more costly than we initially thought. Driven to accomplish, achieve, and attain, we have spent the sum of our time, energy, and mental fortitude attempting to reach for a treasure chest that was empty after all.

America's faith in God has now been replaced by a fear of failure, drive for success, and an undying hunger for more. Our love of money, an unending need for more possessions, and a search for fame have produced exactly what we deserved. We bought into an American dream that couldn't be delivered, or maybe we just interpreted the dream selfishly. Everyone wanted a three-bedroom house with a white picket fence in the cul-de-sac with 2 ½ kids with a golden retriever, but we failed to read the fine print. We've awakened to a world with unemployment, child abuse, school shootings, and homelessness. The pain is real, but our disappointment should have been expected.

While the American dream has led many to prosperity and happiness, others in our country have found themselves in a nightmare of hopelessness and despair. When a child's success in education depends on the quality of his school district or the socio-economical status of his parents, he is likely to never realize the dream. So, we coast through our daily routines like nothing can be done to change our nation's fate. Hope has been minimized to a political slogan, and freedom is held hostage by the loudest complaint in the crowd. American citizens recite the Pledge of Allegiance and sing patriotic songs, but their actions seem more habit than heart. Have we forgotten where we've been? Has our nation lost its soul, or was it all just a dream?

We've forgotten much about our nation's glorious past, but worse yet, I fear we've begun to believe all that we're being told about our nation's future. Freedom has been falling fast, and it appears we've reached rock bottom. Still, I have hope that we're still dreaming, and perhaps the answer will be found as America rises from its slumber. We've been sleeping far too long, but we can still choose to wake up. This nightmare can end here and now, and our best days can still be ahead of us. Hope remains, but the only hope for a world turned upside down is a church turned inside out.

Unending Want (Never Enough)

The American people have become extremely selfish and self-centered in their decisions, positions, and practices. Sadly, we're all in the same boat; Christians are just as guilty as unbelievers. Consider Psalm 37. We appreciate the promise of verse 4 when it says, "he will give you the desires of your heart," but we ignore the three-fold command of verse 7, "be still…wait patiently…do not fret." We all want to enjoy the desires of our hearts without patiently waiting on God to work. How can we possibly know what it means to "delight in the Lord" when our every thought is about us? We miss His best for us because we fail to position Him as our highest priority.

Take the utilitarian pursuit of pleasure and combine it with a misinterpreted American dream of materialism, then top it off with an increased access to easy credit and you get a perfect cultural tsunami. "The inflation in credit leads to inflation in self-image, helping the narcissism epidemic spread far and wide. Take a culture that promotes self-admiration through buying things you can't really afford, and many people live the narcissistic illusion that they are wealthy, successful, and special."[19] Perhaps materialism has always been a problem. Haven't we always been tempted to be greedy and want for more? Consider this one example of how the problem has worsened. A survey of high school seniors in 1976 revealed that 16% considered earning a lot of money as being "extremely important." Compare those findings to a recent survey of 18 to 25-year-olds who were asked to name the most important goal of their generation, to which 81% answered, "becoming rich."[20]

Yes - this social tsunami has been destructive, and the clouds of materialism stretch as far as the eye can see.

Discontentment and envy rule the day in America. But what is envy anyway? The source of envy is our personal lust for more stuff, thinking that somehow more things will translate into lasting satisfaction. But the problem remains; our discontentment - our constant thirst for more - is unquenchable. You know the drill. Something good happens to someone, and your immediate thought is, "I wish that would have been me." This feeling moves quickly from envy, to jealousy, which turns to resentment. Envy wants something, while begrudging someone else for having that same thing. Still the foundation of envy is discontentment. What we have been given is simply not enough to satisfy us, and so we want more and more and more.

Consider this definition from Craig Groeschel, "We see what someone else has, and we want it for ourselves. If we think that we deserve the object of our desire more than the person who has it, our envy blossoms into jealousy. In either case, we are polluting our souls with spores of discontentment that will bloom into lust, avarice, and greed. Put simply, envy is when you resent God's goodness in other people's lives and ignore God's goodness in your own life."[21] Socrates called envy, "the filthy slime of the soul; a venom, a poison, which consumes the flesh and dries up the marrow of the bones."[22]

So, what has caused this problem? First, the American people have a major problem with envy and discontentment simply because they have an elevated estimation of themselves. At our core, we feel entitled. While this undesirable characteristic is present in us all, it is obviously more prevalent in some than others. The risk is that we are unaware of our own problem because we see it so much more in the people around us. This next statement may hurt some of us like a good old shot from the doctor. Listen carefully. Don't miss it.

No matter what you've been given from God...
You don't deserve it!

WHAT? "What don't I deserve?" Truthfully, we don't deserve any of it! We are all unworthy of everything we have. EVERYTHING! Listen to the words of Paul in Romans 12:3: "For by the grace given me I say to everyone among you not think of himself more highly than he ought to think, but to think with sober judgment, each according to the measure of faith that God has assigned." If we all got what we deserved, we would be eternally separated from God in a place called Hell. This is what makes the gospel so beautiful. Jesus died for unworthy sinners, not righteous saints (Romans 5:8). Yet we get lost in the day to day and start believing the hype, assuming the best and forgetting the worst about ourselves.

Don't get me wrong. Christians should have great confidence, but not in themselves. We have confidence in Christ, having nothing to brag about apart from the grace of God and the cross of Jesus Christ. Paul says it like this in Galatians 6:14, "But far be it from me to boast except in the cross of our Lord Jesus Christ, by which the world has been crucified to me, and I to the world." You are at risk of envy and discontentment when you have an unrealistic view of your life, circumstances, and salvation. We tend to see the "many things" we don't have when we take our eyes off of the one thing that actually matters in life, the work of Jesus on the cross.

Americans need a good dose of contentment, a shot of sincere satisfaction. It's so easy for us to obsess on the "*Not Yet*" and miss the "*Already*." Of all people on the planet, Americans are blessed beyond measure. While we're wired to think about our goals and what we're reaching for tomorrow, consider for a moment what you already have in your possession today. Did you know that there are 783 million people in the world who do not have access to safe drinking water? That's more than twice the number of people who live in the United States! And globally speaking, one out of every five deaths of children under five years old is due to a water-related disease.[23] This is just one simple example of many that remind us of this obvious reality. We are blessed beyond comparison, and yet we Americans spend most of our time complaining about how uncomfortable we are in our luxury.

The Christian church has always held the key to the door of contentment, but we have somehow misplaced the key ourselves. What is this key? GOD ALONE IS ENOUGH TO SATISFY MY SOUL. Ultimately, envy is a lack of trust and contentment in God's provision for us. We can't be satisfied in Him and envious of others at the same time. We must learn to truly trust God in everything. He is good, no matter the circumstance, not matter the struggle. God hasn't abandoned us, and He has not made one mistake along the way.

Consider Proverbs 3:5-6: "Trust in the LORD with all your heart and do not lean on your own understanding. In all your ways submit to him, and he will make straight your paths." The NLT says, "Seek His will in all you do." The NKJV puts it like this: "In all your ways *acknowledge* Him." Internalize this truth; God is good to you. Bless His Name! He is worthy of our trust. He is worthy of our contentment. God forbid we become discontented by the distractions of this world. To "acknowledge Him in all your ways" means to actually believe that He has been so good to us.

How do we forget His goodness? How do we become ungrateful? It's easy to look through a clouded lens of selfish foolishness and miss this truth of God's goodness and grace. We are blessed by a loving God, and He is a Good Father who is perfect in every way. He owes us nothing, yet He is always faithful to provide for our every need. We need not wait for another gift to declare His goodness to us. No further proof is needed. The evidence is all around us. God is good, not because of the things He does but for the God that He is. He defines goodness. Envy is our enemy, but God is enough to satisfy our souls. We have the distinct honor to glorify God. Piper said it best, "God is most glorified in me when I am most satisfied in Him."[24]

Undeliverable Promises and Unreasonable Expectations

Have you ever awakened from a good dream only to wish you could go back to sleep and see what happens? In some ways this has become the norm for most Christians in America. We live in the land of semi-consciousness, hoping to catch a glimpse of some synthetic satisfaction. While dreams usually carry a positive connotation, we also understand that every dream carries the potential of turning into a nightmare. That is exactly what has happened to many people in America. We drifted off into dreamland only to wake up in a cultural nightmare. We've brought this on ourselves by dreaming for the wrong things, hoping these earthly possessions could somehow satisfy us in the end. But now we've seen the truth. The light is shining in the shadows, and we see the world's promises for what they really are, a self-serving scam.

I've heard this all my life – "If it sounds too good to be true, it probably is." Well, we've all been served some attractive Kool-Aid, and most of the American people drank it. Some of the message is true. This is the land of opportunity, and hard work does pay off. But the message changed over the years to include a trend toward entitlement and selfish gain. Everyone expected equal pay without equal work, and people started believing this American dream was somehow an inalienable right, not an undeserved privilege. Then others made the dream an idol, lifting it up as their primary goal in life. In the end we should have known better than to think that true satisfaction could be found in a materialistic dream.

We know full well that God will not bless a man who puts something or someone above Him. Jesus taught us, "No one can serve two masters, for either he will hate the one and love the other, or he will be devoted to the one and despise the other. You cannot serve God and money" (Matthew 6:24). Money is not the root of the problem, but our dependence on money can definitely become idolatry. You've probably heard the question, "Are you controlling your money, or is your money controlling you?" The answer to that question ultimately affects everything else in your life, and this is an issue of the heart.

Scripture warns us to guard our hearts. "Do not love the world or the things in the world. If anyone loves the world, the love of the Father is not in him. For all that is in the world—the desires of the flesh and the desires of the eyes and pride in possessions—is not from the Father but is from the world. The world is passing away along with its desires, but whoever does the will of God abides forever (1 John 2:15-17).

Still, even the most committed Christians are constantly tempted to surrender their hearts to lesser things. Materialism has become the new god of the American people. Our money would accurately read, "In stuff we trust." Personal possessions are now our primary concern, and as a result the American dream has become a nightmare. People who approached this challenge with an entitlement mentality were left confused by their self-centered worldview. We soon learned that everyone couldn't have everything. Many were surprised to discover that plans can change, jobs can be undependable, and fortunes can be lost in a moment. Material possessions will never deliver true satisfaction.

Others who sought fulfillment and satisfaction in their possessions quickly realized the emptiness of it all. While earthly possessions and monetary gain may bring a temporary thrill and faux security, they cannot satisfy the longing of a man's soul for true significance. So should we stop dreaming? The problem is not the act of dreaming but the object of our dreams. Our Father is not willing to take second seat to anyone or anything. He deserves our total worship. We are called to, "You shall love the Lord your God with all your heart and with all your soul and with all your mind" (Matthew 22:37).

Ask yourself this question. Which captivates you more, the Provider or the provision? Paul puts things in perspective in Romans 9:20. "But who are you, O man, to answer back to God? Will what is molded say to its molder, 'Why have you made me like this?'" It's fitting to take Paul's statement one-step further. What are we thinking? How could we be given so much by a gracious God and at the same time love the things He gives us more than God Himself? They may call it a dream, but the fraudulent appeal of materialism leads directly to a nightmare that ultimately separates us from the one perfect source of true satisfaction, Jesus Christ.

CHAPTER FOUR
JENGA NATION

We have discussed several challenges that have contributed to the current cultural crisis, including the loss of a moral standard, the universal narcissism of the American people, and the empty extreme of the American dream. Scripture speaks to these in terms of rebellion, selfishness, greed, envy, and pride. These and other factors have lead to an undeniable fracture in the foundation of the nation we love. Some of these public fault lines have come as a result of an aggressive anti-Christian agenda that has been growing in America for decades, but the greatest tragedy is the vulnerability of the individual believers who have lost their strength to stand.

You may have played the game Jenga, or at least seen it on a shelf in the store. The concept is simple. Hasbro refers to it as a "block-stacking, stack-crashing" game, which pretty much sums it up. The idea is to construct a tower of blocks, and then take turns removing them one by one until someone causes the tower to fall. The integrity of the structure is compromised more and more every time a block is removed. The foundation becomes weaker as gaps increase, and stability is inevitably lost. The inevitable result of the self-inflicted structural vulnerability is complete collapse.

Foundational Fault Lines

The explanation of this game could easily be a description of our nation's spiritual condition. We've been playing a game with God, and we're losing more and more every day. The United States was undeniably founded on a set of Judeo Christian values such as the worth of human life, a high regard for marriage, and our responsibility to show compassion to others. However, these building blocks, that once provided stability to our national integrity, are being removed from the public square. This begs the question, "Are these blocks really the foundation?" I don't want to underestimate the significance of our spiritual heritage that can be seen in virtually every document of the founding fathers. We are who we are today, in large part, because of their wisdom to establish a clear public dependence on God.

But allow me to ask this. Which holds more potential for impact on the spiritual climate in America today, the past statement of our founding fathers or the current commitment of a 21st Century Christian? Which is more valuable today, the past voice of a man who made a difference THEN, or the present voice of a man/woman who desires to make a difference NOW? I would suggest the silence of modern Christians is much more detrimental to the integrity of our Jenga tower. Our silence creates vulnerability. Interestingly, our collective voices raised would likely drown out those few who insist on removing the historical markers of such influential leaders. So in the absence of a clear Christian voice, the blocks continue to fall, and the Jenga nation leans further and further towards its inevitable ruin.

While most believers would argue for the preservation of Christianity's influence on the founding fathers in American history, Paul reminds us that it is the church, not our nation's history that serves as "a pillar and buttress of the truth" (1 Timothy 3:15). So what is the answer? What or who is it that holds claim to this most important foundational title? The answer might surprise you. The foundation of the truth, and the answer to America's fault lines, is the church of the living God. Ironically, though it is the solution to our nation's deepest divisions and deficiencies, the church has recently become a major part of the problem, attracting more controversy than converts and ultimately becoming a stumbling block to the very gospel it's been called to promote.

Inevitably the church spends a large portion of its time and energy arguing with lost people, and some would cite this as evidence of the church's faithfulness. After all, Jesus promised persecution would come (Matthew 10:16-25), and there are some legitimate examples of this type of persecution in our day. However, there is also an extreme segment of the evangelical community that considers it their life's primary purpose to aggressively argue with sinners about moral issues in the culture. Congressman Trey Gowdy recently made a strong statement after announcing his retirement from politics. He said, "No one has ever been argued into changing his/her position. You might be loved into it or persuaded into it, but you're never humiliated into changing your position."[25]

I believe much of our frustration has come as a result of lowering ourselves into a fight that can't be won. Our culture provokes us to engage on a war of words on every debatable issue, but these small peripheral battles have often served as distractions from the main event. It's tempting to spend most of our time reading discouraging articles and hateful comments about Christians. It can be addictive to play the role of victims and embrace the culture war as one in which we must fight FOR Jesus, but this is just not a biblical perspective on our calling.

The Old Testament story of Israel's "battle" at Jericho draws a clear parallel to our calling and confrontation of culture. We find the story in Joshua 5:13-15 where the "Commander of the Army of the Lord" meets Joshua face to face. The whole point of this prelude to the battle is that God would be fighting the battle as long as they remained obedient to the call. His instructions were strange to say the least, and there would be no opportunity for an aggressive campaign. Think about it. Joshua was a trained warrior, but he was being instructed to march, blow some trumpets, and shout.

What might have happened if Joshua had taken matters into his own hands? What if he had grabbed a sword and charged the walls of Jericho in force, ignoring the instructions of the Commander? He could have been on the right side and lost the battle for lack of obedience. In fact, Joshua questioned the Commander in verse 13, asking him, "Are you for us or against us?" The answer had to puzzle the soldier, "Neither." But consider the simplicity and significance of this point that we still get wrong today. God is not on America's side! I know that almost sounds like blasphemy, but it's true. God has not blessed our nation because we are entitled to special treatment. We have experienced divine favor because we have founded our nation on biblical principles. We haven't been perfect, but we have acknowledged God's will and way for us enough to benefit from the results. While we strategize and pray for God to help America, to bless "our" plans, He has a plan of His own, and our degree of blessing will be determined by our alignment to His side. No, God is not on our side…but we'd better be on His.

This seemingly small difference is much of our nation's problem in the 21st Century. Jesus offered a very clear commission in Matthew 28:18-20, and this is the equivalent of the instructions to Joshua. But didn't the apostles have occasions of debate and defense of the gospel? Yes, but the question is one of priority of calling. Which is the primary purpose of the church, to win arguments or win souls? The apostles often took an apologetic posture, just as Joshua fought many battles with his sword. However, Joshua was continually reminded who was providing the strength behind his victories, and he also placed obedience to the plan of God as his top priority. This is the challenge for the church in the 21st Century: We've grown too dependent on our own ability to fight the battles, and the walls are not falling anymore.

The Marriage of Faith and Politics

Much has changed in the past few decades in relationship to faith and politics. The American people have increasingly become both obnoxious and obstinate on virtually every side of every issue. While representatives from opposing viewpoints have traditionally been willing to discuss their differences in a civil manner, dialogue and discourse have now died in the public square. Sadly, people of faith are just as guilty as anyone else. While many factors could be blamed for this development, one observation is undeniable. Many Christians have repositioned their priorities, making faith subject to their politics. Like a frog in a kettle, these well-meaning believers don't see the problem. They think they're defending the legitimacy of Christian morality, but in the end it may be their reputation that puts the final nail in the coffin.

Faith and politics are truly inseparable in our personal lives, but it has become popular to compartmentalize beliefs, leading many to possess dueling convictions. While it's reasonable to assume that a person of sincere faith will make political decisions founded on his/her spiritual principles, it's now a foreign concept to most Americans. Unfortunately, somewhere along the way Christians on all sides have sold their souls to the political system. One side neglects faith's influence on their political decisions altogether, while others manipulate their Christianity to promote a political agenda, using faith as a disguise for true motives. Both approaches are wrong. The first would be the equivalent of Joshua refusing to march around the walls and blow the trumpets, while the second would be more like Joshua charging the walls of Jericho in complete ignorance of the Commander's instructions.

Countless politicians have referenced their faith and quoted scripture over the years, but many just use the church as a stage for their own personal promotion. As a result, every political cycle brings another headline that declares the political platform of evangelicals and spotlights a stereotypical "good ole boy" political-pastor. Unfortunately, America's opinion of the church has not been shaped by their passion for social justice, or their compassion for hurting people, or even their hope in Jesus Christ – but their political agenda. Conviction has often turned into compromise, and the world has seen the church...not marching around the walls, but charging the gates with swords drawn. Sure, we're making a lot of noise, but not much progress. We assume God is on our side, but we've forgotten that He's the one in charge.

There are plenty of hostile secularists who have clear agendas to move our nation away from any form of Christian influence. This secular assault on Judeo Christian values provokes a counter-reaction from many who desire to defend the faith foundations of our nation. While it's hard to imagine, we have seen outspoken Christians on both sides of virtually every political issue for decades. From Rev. Jerry Falwell's Moral Majority, to Rev. Jesse Jackson's Rainbow Coalition, it is clear that people can claim to represent Christian values and be on different sides of the fight. While Christians have a responsibility to be engaged in the political process, the marriage of faith and politics has come at a high price.

Prioritized Purpose

Perhaps this is the greatest question. Who has the authority to determine what political issues are "Christian Issues?" Inevitably, marriage skews our view. My wife, Amy, may be aware of my faults, but she will defend me against anyone who criticizes. We tend to see the best in those we love the most. In the same way, this marriage of faith and politics has caused many well-meaning believers to ignore the obvious inconsistencies in their political positions. Again, this is not a one-sided issue. Christians on both sides have defined the issues differently, and errantly compromised on other important matters in order to toe the party line. Sadly, brothers and sisters in Christ have vilified one another for the sake of politics. This is one of the greatest tragedies of modern Christianity, and it needs to change.

Depending on whom you ask, a Christian should be passionately working to reclaim the rights of unborn babies, strengthen the biblical family, promote concern for the poor, ensure the nomination of conservative justices, protect our religious liberty, warn of the dangers of drugs/alcohol, and/or provide for refugees fleeing war-torn nations. If you're like most American Christians, two or three of these issues caught your eye. They are the most important issues to you. And you're right! They are important, but not important at the exclusion of other issues that God cares about equally.

Sadly, many conservative evangelical leaders have begun to vilify promoters of social concerns for fear of doctrinal liberalism. They errantly claim that advocacy for social justice is incompatible with gospel truth. Compassion, however, is not dependent on compromise. Social concern does not equal doctrinal concession. Gospel truth compels us to both share and care. The gospel is the only hope for this world's problems, which all ultimately stem from sin. To claim possession of the true gospel while rejecting the pain of injustice in this world is to align oneself with those spoken of by the Apostle Paul in 2 Timothy 3:5, "having the appearance of godliness, but denying its power." Now, I want to make myself clear. Meeting one's physical needs should never come at the cost of gospel truth, but compassion is not dependent on compromise.

While lines have been clearly drawn between Democrats and Republicans, it's important to remember that God did not draw these lines. I don't know anyone who would say politics should supersede faith in their life priorities, yet many choose to see the best in their political party and the worst in their Christian brother, trading their faith convictions for their political victories. This has definitely left a bad evangelical taste in the mouths of most non-Christian Americans. The Christian's agenda is perceived by most to be political, not missional in nature. "So often in 2018 America, 'evangelical' is associated more with Iowa caucuses than with the empty tomb."[26]

Michael Breznau recently wrote, "The Bible should be our north star when it comes to political belief and practice. And if that is true, then Christians will adopt a political philosophy that is sometimes more conservative than conservatives and at other times is more liberal than liberals. Rather than calling for the development of a 'truly Christian' political party, let's embrace this reality: Christians are political exiles."[27] This openness makes some of us feel very uncomfortable, but it's refreshingly biblical. Jesus never called us to be Democrats, Republicans, or Independents. He called us to be followers, faithful disciples.

Can we just be honest? Some people reading this book care more about politics than people. Many of us are more concerned with winning a political debate than we are about winning a soul for Jesus. We pull a Jega block out of the conversation, but seem surprised when the relational tower falls. I've never seen anyone come to Christ through a political debate, but I have seen many men and women lose their gospel influence while fighting about less important things.

The Pastor, the Pulpit, and Politics

Many people protest a pastor's right to speak to political issues from the stage of a church, but a pastor has the responsibility to faithfully preach on biblical issues. While this may seem like a needless distinction, this one word makes all the difference in the world. Pastors, Christians, and churches in general must speak to issues of social injustice and moral decay, but we must do this from a BIBLICAL perspective. It's a challenge to faithfully speak to issues of scriptural importance without becoming clouded by a particular political platform. Many have made the mistake of placing politics over faith, which inevitably leads to the loss of their influence entirely. A conservative pastor with a political agenda can be just as biblically inept as a liberal pastor teaching from a self-help book.

If a political issue is addressed in scripture then it becomes a biblical one. If the political issue cannot be found in scripture – the pastor should not minimize his voice to the level of a distracting subject that has nothing to do with the gospel mission to which he has been called. A pastor loses his prophetic voice when he prostitutes the pulpit for political purposes. The gospel is minimized by political compromise, and the pulpit is brought down to the level of a campaign spokesman. A pastor should never endorse a candidate or identify himself too closely with a particular party, and he must certainly not defend or condone the immoral actions of a politician. To do so confuses his ultimate allegiance and will likely repel those who may otherwise see Christ in him. Regardless of the issue or party, you lose a significant amount of influence with approximately half the nation when you get political.

Sadly, many pulpits now rest on the platform of a political party, neutralizing their impact on a lost world. A pastor may help a candidate win an election, but he loses his voice in a culture that is constantly turning away from God. Some may say this is the pastor's responsibility, to speak out and change the culture with his influence. I would argue that our influence doesn't have the power to change the culture, and if our mission strategy is founded on overpowering the lost world by shoving them into the box of Christian morality, we have already lost the gospel for it's no longer our message. The GOSPEL "is the power of God for salvation to everyone who believes" (Romans 1:16), NOT the words and policies of men. The gospel is not to be lowered to the level of political propaganda, nor is the agenda of a politician worthy of gaining top priority in any pastor's life.

Political parties shift in platform, and no candidate's character deserves a pastor's public endorsement. They may change positions mid-term, or make a major mistake while on the campaign trail or in office. At the end of the day, a pastor who chooses to become political makes an intentional decision to immediately reduce his audience by 50%. I completely understand and manage this tension on a regular basis. There have been occasions when I have spoken directly to an issue or a politician's statements, but never in an effort to move people politically. A pastor's heart must always be bent toward a gospel goal, a prophetic purpose...not a political one.

Our Greatest Allegiance

American Christians are not called to a political party, and no one group holds the exclusive rights to the "Christian vote" in this nation. Politics cannot save us, and neither Democrats nor Republicans hold the keys to our future hope as Americans. Christ is the only hope for this nation! "And there is salvation in no one else, for there is no other name under heaven given among men by which we must be saved" (Acts 4:12). Like the game of Jenga, many continue to attempt to remove the foundational blocks that have traditionally made our nation strong, but no one can truly remove a Christian's foundation. In Ephesians 2:19-22, Paul calls Jesus our "chief cornerstone," reminding us that He is the one who provides our ultimate stability. Jesus Christ deserves our complete allegiance.

While it's encouraging for a church to display an American flag and sing a patriotic song on July Fourth weekend, church leaders must be careful not to leave room for confusion related to where their ultimate allegiance lies. The church must make much of Jesus! Yes, we are proud to be Americans, but our eternal hope is not in our earthly citizenship. We are foreigners in this Jenga land; this is not our home (Ephesians 2:19 and 1 Peter 2:11). As followers of Jesus we must never forget that our greatest goal, our highest calling, and our ultimate priority is the Kingdom of God (Matthew 6:33).

CHAPTER FIVE

8-TRACKS AND IPHONES

The Generational Divide

So America's foundations have been shaken by the loss of a clear moral standard, leading everyone to seek his own way. While we've been known for decades as a nation who cares for hurting people, it's now every man for his narcissistic self. We can't seem to wake up from this American nightmare, continuing to dream of the money and material things that will bring emptiness in the end. How could this get any worse? The only thing worse than a generation turned upside down is two generations turned upside down, but this doesn't have to be our legacy. Do we love our children and grand children enough to stop this tragic trend?

Yes, our American states seem more divided every day, and this tendency toward separation has seeped into the culture of our churches as well. Truly multi-generational churches seem to be a thing of the past. Any church that is intentionally seeking to effectively reach both 7 and 70 year olds is the exception, not the rule in the 21st Century. The key word is "effectively." Many churches have maintained the stated goal of reaching everyone, but their methods and strategy for ministry reveal the insincerity of their claim. The truth is, it's not easy to target all age groups. Otherwise, every church would do it. Why is it so difficult to reach multiple generations of people today? The answer is not usually a case of spiritual immaturity. Instead, we are most often victims of our own generational uniqueness.

Age is an obvious categorical distinction in our culture. Immeasurable research has been done on the various age divisions in America. By now, we're all familiar with generational labels such as Baby Boomers and Millennials. While there is a wide range of definitions and descriptions of each of these generational categories, most people do accept the existence of such categories and the validity of the impact their evolution has had on our society. These categories should not be seen as universal descriptions of every person in the respective range, but they can be trusted to offer some general tendencies and expectations related to each group.

Every generation has its own general preferences in apparel, communication, music, entertainment, teaching/learning style, culinary habits, occupational practices, charitable giving, financial obligations/investments, social standards, and the list goes on and on. For example, virtually everyone receives the news at some point, but we don't all get the news from the same source. A person's age determines in large part where he gets the headlines. Not many people under 50 years of age are subscribing to the local paper, and Builders aren't exactly flocking to the Internet for online headlines.[28]

This is significant for many reasons, one being the evolving personalization of our online experience. Social media, news apps, and even advertisers are intentionally customized for us based on our past online tendencies. This means we are generally exposed only to the things we are predicted to appreciate. In many ways, those who get their information exclusively online will hear only what they want to hear. This further divides the generational categories, making it even more difficult for the various age groups to relate to one another.

Our American culture has become more and more age-specific in the daily activities of the population. Very few experiences are prepared for the entire family anymore. In most cases, one age group is forced to yield to the other in order to have a shared experience. For example, most adults would prefer not to go to Chuck E. Cheese to celebrate their own birthday, but they would likely be fine hosting their child's party there. Most environments nowadays are catered to one particular target market, which could be any number of sub groups among five very unique generational categories.[29]

Modern marketing strategies all suggest that you must determine a very specific generational target group. Think about it for a minute. Those toy commercials at Christmas time are not geared towards the parents, but the kids. And the prescription drug industry doesn't consider a teenager's preferences when preparing a commercial for an arthritis medication. You can easily determine the target group of any commercial simply by evaluating the content. Every generation and subgroup within that generation has unique preferences, expectations, and motivations that drive their decisions.

This marketing trend has led to even more separation, causing entire communities to gravitate toward and cater to one particular age group demographic. Retirement communities are a good example of this for senior adults, while Snap Chat is predominantly driven by younger generations. Builders, Boomers, Generation X, the Millennials, and Generation Z, all see things differently. These various age groups can be attracted to the same cause or community, but they will not be attracted by the same means or method. To ignore this reality is to unconsciously become fixed on one generation.

There are many benefits to this generational evolution, but we also feel the negative impact it brings to our messaging. Our ignorance and inflexibility have inadvertently created obstacles between the young and the old. How many young boys are listening to older men tell stories of their childhood? How many old men are still willing to tell their stories? Everyone is in his own generational bubble, happy and content to remain isolated from the chaos. But at what cost does this comfort come? What are we losing? Only time will tell, but it seems the answer is obvious. America is losing itself.

Multi-gen Church?

Our generational differences are obvious, and they impact everything we do. Think about it for a minute. A man born in 1950 could have owned a 1966 Mustang, which came standard with an

8-track tape player, and he would have enjoyed having three different choices of shows (Like the Andy Griffith Show) when watching his tube television set that looked more like a piece of furniture than technology. Now consider the young adult born in the late 1990s who can't remember a time in his life when there were no cell phones. In fact, he may barely remember a cell phone that didn't provide internet access and shoot high definition video.

Attempting to appeal to these two extremes and everyone in between proves to be an overwhelming challenge, understanding that a man's expression of worship is deeply cultural. The effort required to create a worship environment for this wide a generational demographic eventually became too high a cost to pay for most churches. Many churches began to offer more contemporary options for younger worshipers, which came with mixed reviews. The sad reality remained that even the success stories of multi-styled worship succeeded at the cost of cross-generational community.

The church where I serve as pastor is one such example. We currently offer three different styles in four services in two locations. We have to be intentional to maximize the distinction of each service, while continuing to value the differences of each. No one style has a higher value than the other. It's a constant tension to manage to be sure, and we try to be deliberate in our efforts to build community between the services, styles, and locations. Our multisite strategy is also unique in that we are transplanting next generation campuses from a multi-generational central campus. You could say we are launching next-gen rockets from our multi-gen launching pad.

While no church is perfect, multi-generational church models do attempt to keep all ages engaged, connected, and aware of the mutual value of the other. It's essential to continually communicate a mutual generational dependency. That is missing in most churches across America today. Many established churches have given up on the task of reaching the lost in their community, while other next-gen churches have forgotten the wisdom and stability that older believers can bring to the table. What has happened? Quite frankly, most churches have selected a particular sub-culture to be its generational target. Now, they may not use that terminology, and they would all state with passion their desire to reach people of all ages, but their strategy (or lack of strategy) and ministry philosophy speak louder than their printed mission statement.

Who are we trying to reach?

Rick Warren's book, *The Purpose Driven Church*, was required reading for one of my classes in seminary. Warren presented what many called "seeker sensitive" strategies, which challenged the church to consider an uncommon question. He surveyed the Orange County community, asking the residents what it was they wanted in a church. This strategic approach to church planting was unheard of, and many still struggle with it today. For better or for worse, Warren dared to consider the preferences of the prospect he hoped to reach over the opinions of those who were already part of a local church.

Those in opposition to this approach usually argued against any strategy that was based on the opinions of man. They contended that this type approach was not built on a biblical model of worship. Instead, they feared that the church was yielding to the cultural trends of the day at the cost of the gospel, but this was a flawed argument. The irony is that all worship is cultural. Even those who most adamantly opposed Warren's approach had their own cultural preferences in worship style, and they defended those preferences. My goal is not to convince you to embrace Warren's ideas, but to admit we can learn some things from his experience.

Christians must become more intentional in our planning if we hope to reach people who are not like us. We often accomplish very little because we're so closed-minded when it comes to methodology. Believers should be open to new approaches to evangelism, as long as they are faithful to scripture. I've heard people criticize contemporary models of church growth, claiming the "attractional" model is man centered. While I firmly believe we should mobilize the body of Christ to go outside the walls of the church to make disciples, the Bible promotes both a "go and tell" and a "come and see" approach to evangelism (Matthew 28:19-20 and John 1:46). It's not my right to declare one is less biblical than the other. I just want to see people come to faith in Jesus Christ.

Agree with him or not on the details, Warren's strategy was instrumental in developing an intentional plan for reaching unbelievers. Those who have already been saved must recognize the need to surrender their own preferences for the sake of those who have not yet embraced God's amazing grace. This doesn't mean we become like the world, but it does cause us to become aware of the people we say we're trying to reach. Part of Warren's strategy was to identify a target prospect; his was "Saddleback Sam."[30] It was a very specific demographic based on the surrounding Orange County area. Again, the idea was based on identifying a target, discovering the needs and preferences of this target group, and then developing a ministry plan to reach people inside this particular demographic.

This is a missional approach to evangelism. Missionaries have done this for years on the foreign field, attempting to discover specific cultural characteristics of the people they intend to reach. It would be much more challenging for missionaries without the ability to narrow their mission by identifying a distinct subculture then developing a strategy based on the research. The American version of this strategy took a different turn during the 1990s and early 2000s when churches became more intentional in their efforts to reach particular age groups. To be fair, this was likely a result of several factors, but they all boil down to generational preferences. So began the generational segregation of the North American church.

There has always been a generational divide to some degree in the American church. I can remember growing up in a small rural church context, but ministry was intentionally geared toward various age groups even in the 70s and 80s. We've always recognized the reality of generational differences. My church took us kids to campouts and derby car races, but I never raced against a grown man. These activities were geared toward boys my age. Why did my church take this approach to ministry even way back then?

First, we learn differently based on our age and stage of development, and we have recognized this reality for decades. You may think your children are exempt, but the average child will not be able to retain much applicable information from a message/lesson prepared for a group of adults. Many parents desire to develop a philosophy of family worship, but methods must be intentionally geared toward children if this is to be effective. Churches often focus more on producing "adult-like" children than they do developing Christ-like disciples. The top priorities of children's ministry should be to help kids fall in love with Jesus and equip parents to disciple their children.

While the moral behavior of our kids is important, their spiritual transformation is the imperative. So we desire to maximize the impact of the gospel on the lives of the children in our churches by making the message relevant to them where they are. The challenge with this approach is that it demands sacrifice from believers, which requires a high level of spiritual maturity (Romans 14-15). Listen to this challenge from Paul in Romans 15:1. "We who are strong have an obligation to bear with the failings of the weak, and not to please ourselves."

I recently read a blog by Chuck Lawless, where he argued for family worship, claiming "children's church too often becomes nothing but babysitting."[31] I don't intend to debate the legitimacy of either family integrated ministry or an age appropriate children's church, but I do find it refreshing to see someone who at least cares about the subject. The problem is not that churches offer "this" type ministry but don't offer "that" type of program, but instead, the generational crisis is one of complacency.

I firmly believe that anyone who is willing to do whatever it takes to invest in the next generation will be somewhat successful in doing so. The churches that have a dying children's ministry have themselves chosen to kill it. Most churches don't seem to care about the next generation at all. Next-gen ministry doesn't even make it on their missional radar. Ironically, children and teens are likely not even a subject of conversation when they think about the future.

Multi-generational ministry is not easy! That's why most churches aren't trying to do it. Oh they may claim to have a multi-generational heart, but the strategy doesn't match their mission statement. So what ensures success in this effort? First, everyone must see the corporate cause worthy of the personal cost. Second, church members have to see future salvations worthy of present sacrifice. Thirdly, mature Christians need to see the value of leaving a heritage for the next generation. While younger believers should respect and honor their older brothers and sisters, we must lean forward in our missional strategy – hoping to maximize our influence on the next generation of Christ-followers.

No one person can always have it his way in a multi-generational church. The corporate cause has to be given the priority over the personal cost when considering a church for all ages. Somewhere along the way the target strategy miscommunicated the point of it all, leading some to adapt a consumer approach that produced an "It's all about me" mentality. The cost became too high a price to pay for most Christians, and as a result they began to unintentionally target people just like them. So by refusing to target all generations, we inevitably only target our own.

It's hard enough to watch generational divisions increase in our culture, but it breaks my heart to see them infiltrate our churches. I firmly believe this is an avoidable tragedy, but it will require immediate action from us all. At first glance, the first half of the book may seem to be a doomsday report, a list of random problems that have led us to become a culture filled with chaos and confusion. In reality, these are obvious social characteristics that we must first admit exist, and then endeavor to overcome. Yes! The world has been turned upside down, but we can still turn the church inside out.

PART TWO

THE CHURCH TURNED INSIDE-OUT

CHAPTER SIX

DROP THE ROCKS

It's official; we live in a world that's been turned upside-down. We're now familiar with the cultural challenges that have led to the current chaos. Our society has been sliding down the slippery slope of moral relativism for decades, and the influence of the Christian church has been all but nonexistent on this ride. Unfortunately, much of this cultural confusion has crept into the church, rendering it virtually powerless. Though commissioned to carry the cause, Christ followers have suffered the effects of this social slide into moral mayhem. However, I still believe that hope remains for this sin sick world. What can possibly reverse this social trend and bring spiritual awakening to our society? The only hope for a world turned upside down is a church turned inside out.

Two Extremes

It's difficult to know how Christians should respond to this chaos. Believers tend to do one of two things. They either aggressively confront the lost world with militant debates that push people away from Jesus, or they turn their frustrations inward on other Christians. Some people choose both. Many Christ-followers believe they've been called to convert people to adhere to a form of Christian morality, hoping to force the social change necessary to make America the nation it once was. But this approach makes the lost world the target of aggression, when Jesus came to show them of love. This militant "ministry" strategy makes sinners the enemy of the church, yet sinners were the entire reason Jesus came to this world. Consider His words in Luke 5:31-32, "Those who are well have no need of a physician, but those who are sick. I have not come to call the righteous but sinners to repentance."

Christians are surrounded by a wicked world that has no spiritual power to truly live righteously, yet many people expect unbelievers to change because we scream at them. We posture ourselves in an argumentative position, attempting to twist the arms of handcuffed men and women – bound by their own rebellion. We continue as if doing the same thing for an extended period of time might eventually bring a new positive result. This is often referred to as the definition of insanity. While believers must stand for truth, that stand must be wrapped in love. We must drop the rocks! Stop hurling hurt at the world Jesus died for. If Christians tried half as much to promote Jesus as they do promoting their political agenda...we would change the world.

In addition to the Christian militants attacking the lost world in the name of biblical defense, there are compromisers who surrender their convictions completely, assuming there is no real hope for missional success without doctrinal compromise. While Christians must be a living demonstration of God's love, we will never reach the world by diluting the gospel! Watering down the truth is just as bad as casting stones at the guilty. These extremes create a tension that turns brother against brother on a number of theological issues. Orthodoxy becomes relative, and the definition of doctrinal liberalism is unique to every man. And so the battles rage, brother against brother and Christian against the culture. Neither war sanctioned by the King, and both are destructive to the mission assigned to us 2000 years ago.

The only way to reach a world that's turned upside-down is to lead your church to turn inside out!

Message or Mission

So what is the answer? The first step toward turning your church inside out is for Christians to embrace the complete gospel, that is an initial transformation that leads to a subsequent mobilization. Some people are extremely committed to an intellectual understanding of the scriptures, but are not as committed to practically live out the gospel in every day life. Many believers hold the false assumption that missional success can only be a result of doctrinal compromise. The assumption is that any effort to penetrate the darkness with relevant, culturally sensitive methodology renders the Christian, leader, or church heretical. This has led to a perceived separation of evangelism and doctrinal integrity. Many believers seems to do everything they can to discredit and demonize the evangelistic methods of others simply because they themselves are not faithfully reaching out to the lost.

This phenomenon has negatively impacted the unity of the body more than we realize. Consider this scenario that can be found in virtually every town in America. A contemporary church has started in town and is growing rapidly. They do seem to be reaching people who had not previously attended church, but other churches are threatened by the presence of this new "competitor." As a result, Christians in other churches become resistance to anything that resembles the methodologies of the new congregation. Perhaps someone mentions serving coffee in the lobby, and the immediate accusation is that the church is going contemporary, as if contemporary is some other gospel altogether. Some church members jump to ridiculous conclusion at the sight of anything new. This overreaction is not the result of one's doctrinal convictions but fear of personal loss.

It's discouraging when people assume that words like contemporary and modern are synonymous with doctrinally weak. Truly, if your doctrine can be weakened by small methodological adjustments in your worship style or evangelism strategy, it was never strong to begin with. Being traditional in style doesn't make us more spiritual or conservative. There are countless doctrinally liberal churches that are very traditional. Only an ignorant Christian would assume that a music style or a choice in program definitively determines a church's theological positions.

These needless disputes on style and methodology serve as a spiritual smoke screen, preventing us from asking more important questions. Can a man claim to truly believe the message if he is unwilling to embrace the mission? Can a Christian be faithful to both the doctrinal message and the missional method? The answer is yes! Just because you don't do it doesn't make it wrong. When did we start criticizing churches for actually obeying the Great Commission? It's true that some larger churches are doctrinally weak, but there are certainly just as many weak small churches. It's become unthinkable to spotlight smaller churches that have surrendered their calling for comfort. Can we just stop criticizing each other's methods and get back to the mission?

Large churches are NOT the enemy of small churches. The first church I pastored was five miles outside a town of 3,500 citizens and was located a mile from the nearest house. But listen, that church never made excuses, and they've never stopped reaching the lost. A small church can be on mission and be just as evangelistic as a mega church. While the terms and measurements of success may change based on the size of a church, no congregation is exempt from the call to make disciples. So why is it that large churches tend to get a negative reputation? In part, some of them deserve it, but that's not the whole story. Pride, jealousy, and envy are a few words that should be added to the conversation, but all these can be summed up in the word sin.

It's terribly disturbing to hear a "Bible-believing" Christian make excuses for his/her lack of evangelistic passion by bashing the faithfulness of another church. This is unacceptable and ultimately detrimental to the larger body of Christ. Yet it happens all the time. It's so easy for pastors to become self-righteous and begin to sell themselves a pack of lies. We often feed off one another's envy and pride, declaring this church to be weak or that pastor to be soft. How else could they be reaching people when we're not, right? This is a major problem in the church today.

Perhaps it's the constant reminders to the congregation that it's not about the numbers, or maybe you're regularly explaining the challenges you face because of your church's location. Some even slip into a doctrinal pit of excusing away their responsibility to evangelize the lost by stating that it all ultimately depends on God. While salvation cannot and will not happen apart from God's grace and leadership, YOU AND I ARE RESPONSIBLE TO SHARE THIS GOOD NEWS. The church is the vehicle by which Christ is redeeming His people. You're it!

With all due respect, we need to stop making excuses and get to work! God has called us to share the gospel, now, today. We must take our eyes off of that pastor or that church or that ministry, and set our eyes back on Jesus. I challenge you to personally call yourself out. What am I focusing on? We need to repent of pride and covetousness! This has become a cancer in our Christian walk and has prevented our own success in the mission.

Either/Or? – Both/And?

While one church may be extremely evangelistic, baptizing people by the hundreds or even thousands, many people assume such a church makes a conscious choice to exchange doctrinal depth for missional successes. Likewise, when a pastor promotes his strong commitment to discipleship, many immediately jump to the conclusion that he must not be very evangelistic. These are not only ministry myths; they are lies from Satan himself. The issue goes far beyond surface terminology, making it unfair for us to make broad characterizations based solely on unfounded stereotypes.

Why is it that one congregation refuses to celebrate the evangelistic fervor and rapid growth of another? Instead of celebrating life change in other churches, some proceed to make unsubstantiated accusations of doctrinal deficiency or methodological offense. Many people assume that a growing church cannot possibly be teaching the truth. I can't count the number of times I've heard people make derogatory remarks about a church's growth, claiming that compromise is the inevitable source of such success in evangelism. Having said that, I have personally observed weak theology in both traditional and contemporary churches. Shallow doctrine is just as likely in a small church as a large one, and "doctrinal depth" does not mean, "boring." One might think these terms were synonymous, but I agree with Dr. Robert Smith, who says that doctrine should dance.[32]

Why does it have to be either/or? Many believe it's impossible for a church to be both evangelistic and doctrinally sound. I would argue that if you're not being obedient to the call of Christ to make disciples, you're church is likely weaker doctrinally than the one's your throwing stones at down the road. Drop the rocks and pick up a bag of seeds. We've been called to go and sow. Reaching and teaching are inseparable stages of the same missional process.

Why do churches feel forced to choose between evangelism and doctrine? Good doctrine drives the believer to evangelize the lost. This is not an either/or issue. Any biblical approach to this discussion demands we hold a balanced view of these two important tasks. Matthew 28:19-20 clearly lays out the expectation, presenting the Great Commission as a two-part process. Jesus commands His followers to "go and make disciples of all nations, baptizing them" [evangelism]. But He goes on to add the next stage of the command, "teaching them to observe all that I have commanded you."

Christians are not forced to water down their faith in order to be relevant in this culture, and churches don't have to grow at the expense of doctrinal integrity. It's not only possible to simultaneously reach the lost and teach the saved, it's the plan of God. This is the gospel of Jesus Christ. If we believe the message, then we must obey it by living out a disciple-making mission. So the church is called by Christ to reach and teach His followers, to reach and teach new disciples. We are not given an option to pick and choose which part of the commission we prefer or feel most comfortable with. NO! This is what it means to follow Jesus.

Evangelism does not have to come at the cost of doctrinal depth. We don't have to trade one for the other. The end of multiplication is not justified by the means of malnutrition, nor is doctrinal depth so valuable that God provides an evangelism exemption to those who prefer to spend more time in His word. Quite frankly, those who spend time with Jesus will be compelled to share the gospel with others who need it. The air of religious superiority is present in many established churches in America, but so is consumerism packaged in a doctrine-less message. It could go either way, but it doesn't have to. Let's celebrate life-change with doctrinal substance.

Liberals and Legalists

Yes, you can experience multiplication without malnutrition. Your church can celebrate with substance, but it's not easy. Remember, in order to reach a world turned upside down, we've got to turn the church inside out. There seems to always be at least two opposing extremes in any ministry related discussion. Ironically, God's word supports neither. Imagine the Bible in the center of the room, absolute truth, and the standard for all we believe. On the far right is legalism, manmade rules that add requirements to the Bible. On the far left of the room are more liberal opinions that attempt to take away from the Bible's message. So while legalists say the Bible is not enough, liberals say the Bible is too much. Either extreme is heresy!

A church turned inward inevitably becomes filled with self-righteous people who create new rules for everyone else to follow. An inward focused church tends to posture itself in opposition to the world instead of in support of the lost. They construct barriers of defense, minimizing the access many might otherwise have to the gospel message. They create extra-biblical mandates that confuse, if not offend, those far away from God. It's undeniable; the gospel is offensive enough. We need not add unbiblical requirements to our religious expectations. This just creates obstacles to broken people experiencing the grace of God.

A church turned outward at the cost of biblical truth becomes filled with spiritual compromise, attempting to destroy any resemblance of righteousness. A theological liberal embraces the world with open arms, but they drop the Word of God in the meantime. They've convinced themselves they can't carry the truth and care for sinners simultaneously. These people remove barriers that stand between God and sinners, but they somehow forget the need for the gospel along the way. While we don't need additional rules added to scripture, we certainly can't neglect the supremacy of the scriptures.

We must learn to trust the truth. God's Word is enough. He has revealed Himself to us, and nothing has been left out. Do you want to reach unbelievers? Stop imposing a uniform policy of churchgoers. Nothing appears more disingenuous than for the church to have an expectation (even unwritten or unspoken) that cannot be found anywhere in the Bible. This is legalism, and it makes God sick. Do you remember how Jesus referred to the Pharisees who were more concerned about the outside of the cup than they were the inside? Jesus was not happy, calling them "blind guides," and "whitewashed tombs full of dead people's bones" (Matthew 23). That is some tough preaching! Jesus wasn't preaching to the moral failure, but to the men who looked like they were religious elitists.

Ministry is full of stereotypes, both good and bad. I remember early in my ministry hearing legendary preachers make fun of others who chose to preach from a stool and table rather than a pulpit. They belittled virtually any creative tactics, while declaring the conventional way to be the only "legitimate" way to do ministry. Guys like me were easily influenced in those days. All we knew was what these "experts" told us, but deep down I knew the points seemed shallow and empty. I sure couldn't find support for their statements in the Bible they held high in the air. The message was always filled with extra-biblical imperatives, constructed on the opinions and preferences of men rather than the word of God. They would declare these fallacies at the top of their lungs, with passion and fire, as if they were defending the virgin birth. Ironically, this was a weak message in the name of biblical strength, malnutrition in the name of health. It was a neo-liberalism of sorts, traditionalism in the name of conservatism, preferential heresy presented as divine imperative. Sadly, the masses loved it, and this doctrine helped shape a generation of "conservative" preachers in America.

These two opposing extremes are always present, and both are contrary to the word of God. Micah Fries said it best, "Liberalism and legalism are two sides of the same coin. Liberalism masquerades as love, while legalism masquerades as holiness. Still, both are a denial of the sufficiency of scripture. Liberalism says scripture goes too far, while legalism claims it doesn't go far enough."[33] If the church is going to reach this generation we must drop the peripheral preferences and stick to the stuff of scripture. If we are to experience multiplication without malnutrition, we must get back to the Bible and stop playing religious games on these two extremes.

Friendly Fire

We live in a day of Christian tension between the two extremes on numerous issues, and very few people share common opinions on any two issues. Two people may stand shoulder to shoulder on one issue of great importance, but then the next topic is raised. Open hands become closed fists as names are taken, and the fight turns inward. Most debates lead to a frustrating fight where no one really comes out a winner. Oh sure, someone stands holding the trophy or holding the political office, but at what cost? It begs the question, why are we fighting each other? Now I'm not suggesting we refuse to stand up for truth, but I am saying that righteous wars should be limited to our real enemy. Far too often we turn our weapons on our own brothers and sisters, people we agree with on the essentials of the faith. Instead of coming together, we dig more trenches, and we burn more bridges to prove our points. We've grown so accustom to fighting that we can't seem to find peace with ourselves.

The debates abound. Denominational distinction, reformed theology, worship methodology, eschatology, the role of women in ministry, young/old earth, social drinking... these are only a few examples of many peripheral doctrinal issues. Now, depending on whom you ask these examples may be non-negotiable, and that is my point exactly. It's impossible to teach a stubborn man anything, but one's sincerity of conviction doesn't make his belief any more legitimate. Wrong is always wrong no matter how loud, long or proud you believe it to be true. It's interesting to see how convinced people can be in matters that have been disputed for thousands of years by legitimate Bible-believers. How can a man hold up the

Bible in one hand, while shaking his fist with the other, shouting extra-biblical mandates as if they were printed in the black and white pages? The church has lost much if we have lowered our view of scriptural authority to the level of our own personal opinions.

My early years of ministry were bathed in the strongest of conservative influences, and I'm very grateful for that. There were, however, plenty of disappointments along the way. Men I respected lost their voices by tearing down the ministries of others. In the name of conservative theology, many criticized the use of modern techniques and unconventional methodologies, labeling participants to be doctrinally weak or biblically lite. The longer I've been in ministry, the more I've learned that consistency is uncommon among us on the conservative side. It has often been those same pastors who criticized other preachers for their topical sermons, which they'd call "motivational speeches," who themselves fell prey to the same temptation in a different form.

The dangers of this internal warfare cannot be overstated, and it's present on both extremes. Doctrinal categories and subjective terminology continue to drive a wedge between people who serve the same God, believe the same book, and are on the same mission. Far too many of my friends have drawn a line of fellowship in the sand over reformed theology. To declare oneself a Calvinist is to be rejected by one tribe and embraced by another. While I am not a Calvinist, it breaks my heart to see the sinful aggression that results from this discussion. Both sides have formed a militant posture as they hurl the doctrinal rocks. On another battlefield, many faithful believers are labeled advocates of a "social gospel" simply because they live out their faith in the public square. While they believe every word of the Bible, these social servants stand accused of liberalism. Why are they accused? They feel compelled by the gospel to care for less fortunate people, those who have been abandoned and neglected. Like the Pharisees, however, certain "men of God" criticize those who are actually doing the work of God. They have no hands to serve the "least of these" because their hands are full of rocks.

While pastors are not called to be social workers, we are required to love hurting people. That's not liberal, but biblical. Jesus stood up for the vulnerable and the outcasts. How can anyone who has read the Bible ignore that fact? These kinds of extremes are killing the church. We construct manmade categories and predefine the terms, rendering everyone who disagrees with us a heretic. Meanwhile, we ourselves are often the guilty party. Perhaps we're not the ones throwing the stones, but there we stand with Stephen's garments in our hands.

We're on the same side, right? One wouldn't know it from the outside looking in. Everyone knows that if you put ten Christians in a room you'll have at least fifteen opinions because we can't even agree with ourselves most of the time. Disagreements are not bad in and of themselves. In fact, a variety of viewpoints provide multiple opinions, which usually produces a well-informed decision. Our diversity can be our strength as long as we seek unity – not uniformity. Our goal is to agree on the mission, vision, and core values of the ministry, but we should never expect everyone to agree with the process and methods we embrace to pursue our God-given purpose.

This is not a new problem in the faith. Christ Himself challenged His church to love one another (John 13:35), and He prayed for unity among his followers (John 17:21). Paul repeatedly challenged believers to work together in unity, as one body (Romans 15, 1 Corinthians 1 and Ephesians 4). The early church faced constant temptation to allow personal disputes and doctrinal disagreements to divide them, but the heart of Christ has not changed. He still desires that we become one in Him.

All Generations

While we understand that people of various ages and life stages are going to see things from different perspectives, one would think our common faith in Jesus would serve as a sufficient bridge to bring us all together. How do we reconcile these two generational extremes? From suits and ties to shorts and flip-flops – from organs and hymns to lights and haze machines – generational differences are real. I consider it an extreme joy and privilege to serve a church that endeavors to bring the generations together, but there is a reason most churches don't try. It is extremely difficult. In fact, most people would say it's impossible.

I am reminded virtually every day that 80 year olds and 28 year olds see things differently. Should we prohibit wearing hats or drinking coffee inside the Worship Center? Both senior adults and young adults would consider these questions common sense, but would hold to two opposing positions. Should the church make an overtly patriotic emphasis in a worship service? Again, different people see these type of issues from unique perspectives, and generational lines are a big factor. Sadly many churches have decided to avoid this tension by choosing a side, and in essence rejecting one of the generations. This is why you rarely see a church filled with people of all ages. People often refuse to drop their rocks. They have chosen personal preferences over divine purpose.

We understand the cultural challenges of multiple generations attempting to work together, and there are many. But the benefit of success in this area far outweighs the cost of investment. This is worth it guys! Unity in this mission is worth older Christians investing in and empowering younger Christians. This calling to reach the lost requires wisdom from the former generation, and younger men and women need to hear this. YOU DON'T KNOW IT ALL! There is so much you need to learn from the people who have served for decades before you. Yes, one generation wears bow ties, while the other wears ball caps, but we're more alike than you might think.

Beyond the issue of generations coexisting in the church, is the need for balanced generational leadership. This conversation produces an immediate defensive response from many older leaders who feel the younger generation has simply become impatient and is a product of the entitlement culture around us. They would suggest that leadership requires a lot of experience and should not be surrendered to youngsters with visions of grandeur and unconventional dreams. I'm sure glad people didn't think that way in 1776. Consider the ages of these Founding Fathers of the United States of America. On July 4, 1776 Aaron Burr was 20. Alexander Hamilton 21. James Madison 25. Thomas Jefferson was 33. John Adams was 40. George Washington was 44, and James Monroe was 18.

James Madison finished writing the Constitution at the age of 27 years old. Leadership should never been seen as exclusively an older person's responsibility. We desperately need a balance of generational involvement and investment in the process of leadership. Sadly, it's rare to find a church with generational balance. Most congregations focus their attention and energy on pleasing one particular generation at the exclusion of all others. So depending on which corner you're standing on, the church is either growing older or younger. It seems our modern day Elijahs and Elishas have never learned how to serve and lead together, but this has to change!

There are many examples of one generation passing the mantle, including King David and his son Solomon. What about Moses and Joshua? We could find a similar example in the New Testament with Jesus and the twelve disciples, and don't forget the Apostle Paul and his younger mentees Timothy and Titus. These biblical mentors invested in their understudies and prepared them for the approaching transition. God's plan is that we pass the message of Christ on to the next generation, but this is easier said than done. Most transitions in our day are more of a competitive struggle than an intentional succession plan.

This seems to be the end of an inheritance, once filled with hopes and promise, now ending in spiritual bankruptcy - a legacy lost on moral failures, doctrinal divides, and methodological debates. And so the fields remain ready for harvest. Though our fathers have grown older and unable to work the fields as they once did, their children seem to have left the fields entirely. Some say the young have abandoned the work, while others say the older never gave them a chance. And so the blame game begins. We must drop the rocks!

How can we move forward? I challenge the older generation to reject your fear of loss, and embrace an investment mentality. Stop blaming and start claiming the next generation. Get over the debates, and get on your knees before God. The opposite is also true; you need the younger generation. While our physical lives will end soon enough, the legacy of our mission will live forever. Your investment today will determine the promise and inheritance of the next generation. Why would we grasp the mantle with clinched fists, refusing to transfer it to the leaders of tomorrow? Now is the time, and you are the bridge to a missional inheritance. Pass it on!

I'm afraid we've forgotten what makes us ONE. It's most definitely not our worship style or apparel on Sunday mornings. Our unity is not found in our shared political affiliation or in a preaching style that everyone enjoys. No! Paul makes it clear in Romans 12:5, "so we, though many, are one body in Christ, and individually members one of another." We are ONE. Say yes to the future. Don't die with the mantle in your hands. Stop blaming and start claiming the next generation for Jesus. While we pick up the pieces from broken dreams of what might have been, the mission remains before us. Let's dream a new dream of a better day, a vision of unity and oneness. Young/old, modern/traditional, formal/casual – we are The Church.

CHAPTER SEVEN

TRADE SUITS FOR BOOTS

Once Christians have dropped the rocks we will have our hands free to do the work God has called us to accomplish. It's sad to say that believers are often known more for what we're against than what we believe in, and we most often appear to be the enemy of the world Jesus came to save. Unbelievers are always watching, and they have an opinion about everything we do. Stereotypes abound, good and bad. Some are unfair and unfounded, while others are undeniably accurate. One thing is certain, a lot has to change if we are going to reach this generation for Christ.

While we would like to think of our local church facilities as mission centers, the vast majority of churches serve more as an isolated hiding place for Christians to run away from the culture around them. Christians have retreated into social bubbles where we remain comfortable and safe from possible exposure to the contaminated community. This trend has led pastors to gravitate toward an institutional model of ministry that further insulates them from unbelievers. Ministers tend to function more like corporate moguls than missionaries, but this idea cannot be found in scripture. Missionaries choose boots over suits.

Think like Missionaries

You are a missionary! In fact, every Christian is a missionary. This has been true since the resurrection, but it's more obvious now than ever. We love to categorize and prioritize everything. Humans are systematic by nature, and we like to program everything we do. As a result the expectations of local church ministries in North America have evolved over the years to become institutional and programmatic in purpose. This evolution of ministry has led to a redefinition of missions, which has communicated an unhealthy distinction between local church ministry and the foreign mission field.

Foreign missions is an undeniable part of the call of God on every believer, but it's impossible to claim that God has placed a higher value on foreign missions than your personal local mission field. Scripture makes it clear that our mission starts at home and expands to the ends of the earth (Matthew 28:18-20). Jesus lays out a progressing commission in Acts 1:8. "But you will receive power when the Holy Spirit has come upon you, and you will be my witnesses in Jerusalem and in all Judea and Samaria, and to the end of the earth."

I memorized these passages of scripture in my early childhood, but I had a big misunderstanding of what a missionary was. My church had missionaries visit from time to time in an effort to raise awareness and support for their work. I was always interested to learn about a new culture and hear stories about what it was like to live in another country and meet people who speak a different language. These missionaries seemed so different from us, wearing native clothing and showing us exotic items from their mission field. It was awesome! But sadly, I was taught that this was what mission work was all about. The call of the church member was to give them money and pray for the "real missionaries" because they were willing to follow God's calling.

I have the highest respect for vocational missionaries who willingly sacrifice so much by leaving the comfort zone of the U.S. to follow Christ to the ends of the earth, but my view of biblical missions is not limited to these amazing servants of God. God has not exclusively called a group of Special Forces Christians to do all the dirty work of missions. Somehow the work of missions has been redefined to limit it to a vocational branch of ministry, when it's really an all-inclusive part of what it means to follow Jesus. Mission work is not limited by geography, and it's not defined by distance of one's journey. The value of a man's soul does not increase or decrease based on his nationality or the continent on which he lives. Missions anywhere is just as valuable as missions everywhere.

What is the definition of Christian missions? We must agree that missions is not an exclusive calling to a few superior Christians who are willing to sacrifice more than the rest of us. NO! You are a missionary. I am a missionary. Perhaps you live in the Southeast United States or maybe you're out West. Christians live all over the planet, but wherever you happen to be planted by the providence of God, you are called to serve God in that community. You are called to follow Jesus where you are. We are all called to be missionaries – locally, regionally, nationally, and globally.

Consider this. No matter where you live in America, the world has come to you. Mayberry has gone global, and the nations are moving across the street. While it can be intimidating to many, this trend should be seen as divine opportunity, God opening missional doors to His followers. I've been blessed to go on many foreign mission trips, and God has used those global encounters to shake my faith, wake my spirit, and spread His gospel. But our calling to go there does not diminish our responsibility to go here. The example Christ gave us in Acts 1:8 began in Jerusalem and extended to the ends of the earth. I've heard Jonny Hunt say, "The light that shines the farthest, shines the brightest at home." Our calling begins at home, wherever that may be.

Short-term mission trips can definitely be of great value to the kingdom. They offer an important level of support for those who serve on foreign lands, but they also provide an immeasurable benefit to those who travel. Every trip, every nation, every community has had a lasting impact on my life. Still, the heart of a biblical philosophy of missions is not short-term trips but a life-long investment. Our missions investment should never be limited by geography. We are all called to live on mission, every day and everywhere we go. You are a missionary!

My good friend, Keith Shorter recently wrote an article that perfectly sums up this point. He is a long-term pastor and denominational leader, but still admits the struggle we as "non-missionary Christians" have by errantly drawing a distinction between us and them, local church ministers and vocational missionaries. "Missionaries are not tourists; they live on a mission, driven to share the Gospel with those who are living far from God. Their efforts are deliberate; their concern for their city is genuine. I am always challenged by their example and reminded that my church should do likewise."[34]

The purpose of the modern church is not to promote a program or convert people to institutional religious loyalty. We are called to focus on lostness every moment of every day. God forbid we have become Christian tourists in our own communities, lacking a sincere concern for the cities in which we live and neglecting to share the gospel with the lost that live there. We must start thinking like missionaries, but how do we do that?

Study and Adapt to the Culture

What do foreign missionaries do when they're called to serve a particular people group? They learn everything they can about the people they've been commissioned to reach with the gospel. They research the language and customs while attempting to remove any barriers that might be of particular significance to their unique sub-culture. Missionaries recognize that every culture is unique, and we must adapt to the culture that God has called us to impact. Yet when we think in terms of local ministry, many wrongly reject this concept entirely. They don't see the culture as something to learn from, evaluate, and strategically infiltrate. Instead, some see American cultural dynamics to be the enemy of the mission.

There are sub-cultures of various people groups within every larger national culture, including the United States of America. While a majority of foreign missionaries have adopted a culture-centric approach to their efforts, expansion of the church in

North American seemed to take a different approach. Christians created somewhat of a standard model for churches that was reproduced in many communities across the nation. This cookie cutter approach was actually effective with a significant percentage of the population for a specific period of time, but the culture changed. Sadly, most American churches did not change with the culture. The great majority of Christian churches in America have not made the transition into the 21st Century. Should the cultural trends of the 1970's come back, we will experience a mass revival. So we continue using the same methods, speaking the same language, and working the same programs that haven't been effective in decades.

Ironically, many once vibrant churches are now dying in the name of faithfulness to God, but the cause is cultural. While they may see the outside culture of American society to be the enemy, it's the internal church culture that may be the greatest enemy of the mission. We must crack the cookie cutter! Every church has it's own distinct culture, a unique personality. While we proclaim the same gospel, God has made us all different for a reason. A cookie cutter church has a limited reach, and will never effectively impact the lost community outside the walls. It's so easy to become overly focused on the internal needs of the church, and neglect the primary calling of God.

You are a missionary, and your church is a missions organization. The community where you serve is the mission field, and God is calling you to be the unique "you" He has created you to be. You should and must support foreign missions efforts, but not at the neglect of those who live across the street. Look around you! It's not a sin to be culturally minded when considering how to structure your church ministry. It may, however, be a sin to ignore the lost world around you. Churches are complacent, and truthfully many pastors are lazy. Yet we remain stubborn in the name of holiness and tradition. How ironic. We must not disobey the commission in the name of godliness.

Boots Not Suits

Practically speaking, many Christians have limited their sphere of kingdom influence to a small group of believers who meet inside the four walls of a church building one or two days a week for a couple hours. This is unthinkable! We can't afford to compartmentalize the commission. God has called us to impact the neighborhoods in which you live. You are a missionary! We've not been called to live in isolated bubbles of self-righteous comfort. Instead, we need to get out in the community, meeting neighbors and building relationships. Believers are commissioned to build relational bridges to those who are far away from God.

We cannot compartmentalize the commission. You are a missionary, regardless of your occupation. You've been called to go, reach, and teach the people of your community – to make disciple who make disciples (Matthew 28:18-20). For the average Christian this seems an overwhelming responsibility, but our anxiety comes from a self-inflicted confusion. God calls many to a marketplace ministry, leading them to impact and influence those around them, no matter where that is. Christians must begin to see their occupations as missional opportunities. From corporate executives to a middle school teacher, every job is an open door to kingdom influence.

Then we have the matter of vocational ministry in the United States. This is not an indictment on compensating ministers, but what would happen if we started thinking like missionaries? Most vocational missionaries don't sit in an office 40 hours a week. They live with the people they've been called to reach. They get out in the fields, building relationships and investing in local church leaders. We have an obvious problem in the U.S. We have somehow disconnected the church from the world around it. What would happen if we traded our suits for boots? What if ministers got out of the confines of the church office and made intentional efforts to connect with unbelievers. This would be, well, biblical.

One of the major hindrances to effective missions in our day is that we have isolated the missionaries from the mission field. Pastors need to be mobilized to connect with the community, but this will require a shift in priority for most churches. The evolution of American Christianity has led to a mindset of maintenance over mission. We often seem more concerned about pleasing those who are already saved instead of reaching those who remain hopelessly lost. So believers, get out of the church building and get into the community. Build relationships and make connections with people far from God. Build bridges to unbelievers, and stop burning them.

Turn Confrontations into Conversations

This sounds like a bad cliché, but I'm going to say it anyway. We, as Christians, are often our own worst enemy. Surely we recognize the obvious; our real enemy, Satan, is throwing up smoke screens and causing as much confusion as possible in hopes that he might bring on some friendly fire. He wants nothing more than to turn brother against brother, laying casualties along the road of faith. The Devil wants us to fight each other - to discredit one another - to harm one another. But your brother is not the enemy; the deceiver is the real enemy. Satan is a liar, the father of lies, and he is busy casting doubt at every turn (John 8:44). He is a thief who wants to rob you of joy, kill your testimony and destroy any purpose God has for you (John 10:10). And he is good at what he does. As a result, Christians spend more time arguing with other believers then we do sharing the gospel with unbelievers.

Listen, this nation is our home, but as Christians it's also our mission field. It's a battlefield too, but our enemy target is not other believers nor is it other Americans. We're not even fighting against other people! We must draw a clear distinction between the true enemy and those we hope to reach. We can't reach out a hand to help our brother out of a pit until we've laid down the hammer that we hold. While, as believers, we often walk through our daily lives oblivious to the spiritual battle around us, we live in a constant tension of cause and chaos. Paul attempts to teach us this truth in his letter to the Church at Ephesus. "For we do not wrestle against flesh and blood, but against the rulers, against the authorities, against the cosmic powers over this present darkness, against the spiritual forces of evil in the heavenly places." Ephesians 6:12

Does your church desire to make a significant kingdom impact in this generation? Do you as a Christ follower want to reach lost souls with the gospel? If so, stop fighting people and start loving them. The world is upside-down, and they need a church that is inside out. We must turn unnecessary confrontations into gospel conversations. I challenge you to make the intentional decision to engage people in a sincere dialogue. I know it sounds crazy in our day, but it's not a sin to talk about important issues with people you disagree with. Christians are not generally greeted with open arms by the secular American culture, but it's not all the world's fault. We've brought much of the negative public opinion on ourselves over the years.

Christians have to learn to listen as much as we talk, and be willing to have a conversation with people who disagree with us. It's not wrong to listen to the points of view from people with whom you completely disagree. Truthfully, Christians often sound foolish because we're uninformed on issues. This may be because we're not silent long enough to hear the voice of those in opposition to our views. Let's hit the pause button on our prepared talking points, and try to hear the heart of those on the other side from time to time. Instead of immediately jumping to conclusions and assuming the worst, pray that God would use us to build a bridge of grace instead of burning it down. Make the decision to sit down and talk, actually have civil dialogue, a thought provoking exchange of ideas. God will use our humility and grace to draw men and women to himself.

Focus on Rescue not Survival

With internal focus comes a survival mentality. A church that is constantly worried about keeping its members happy and maintaining the status quo will never accomplish a God-sized vision. While members should never be ignored or neglected, senior leaders should teach them that this faith journey is about sacrifice.

Jesus Himself, God in flesh, left Heaven and came to earth in order to serve unworthy sinners.

"...whoever would be great among you must be your servant, and whoever would be first among you must be slave of all. For even the Son of Man came not to be served, but to serve, and to give his life as a ransom for many." Mark 10:43-45

How can we as sinners consider ourselves more deserving of comfort and preference than the perfect Son of God? It's not about you! Remember how clear Jesus makes this point in Luke 5:32, "Those who are well have no need of a physician, but those who are sick. I have not come to call the righteous but sinners to repentance." Are we called to care for believers in their distress and pain? Absolutely! This internal care is an important part of our ministry, but NOT the primary focus to which God has called us. Jesus again teaches us to willingly leave the large crowd to find the one lost sheep (Matthew 8). If forced to choose between maintenance or mission, the church that has turned inside-out is already positioned and prepared to find the lost sheep. The mission is the primary purpose of the people.

We are not a boat in distress, fighting back the waves for fear of being toppled over in the deep. We are not in survival mode! We are the searching ship. The church is sending our team of rescuers, looking for others who are vulnerable to the elements of this world, alone in the dark, afraid for their lives. The church truly is their lighthouse, and we are called to a rescue mission. Imagine a Navy Seal diving in dangerous waters to pull vulnerable victims from a threat of a raging storm. It is unfathomable to consider that such a sacrificial servant would stop to complain about how uncomfortable it was to get water in his ears. Why? He is on a mission. It's what he's been prepared for, the purpose for his existence.

What if the call for help came to the Navy Seal and he responded by saying he would head the victims' direction immediately after the baseball game is over. "It's just not a convenient time right now." This is a ludicrous scenario, but it's because the man's purpose demands a particular response. It's why he exists, the reason he has trained and prepared. It's not just a job; it's the Seal's identity. You too have been called to a sacrificial purpose. When someone is lost in sin, we don't debate if it's convenient or comfortable to attempt a rescue. Rescue is more than what we do; it's who we are.

The church is called to love the world, hurting people who are far away from God. We are the body of Christ, called to love people the way He loved them. This is not the current state of Christianity. A recent article in the Washington Post exposed an extreme inconsistency in American evangelicalism. Research shows that those who are religiously unaffiliated are more likely to be concerned about the wellbeing of refugees than Evangelical Christians in the United States.[35] I acknowledge that surveys are often skewed by the political agenda of those asking the questions, but this is bad news either way. Regardless of our political position on any related issue, a Christian's heart should always break for hurting people. We must make the commission of Jesus Christ our highest priority, yes even over our politics. Our goal is rescue, not survival.

Transformation, Reconciliation, and Representation

We've established the importance of studying the culture and people we plan to serve, but our theology is equally important. One could learn all there is to know about the geography, history and language of the people preparing to effectively deliver a message, but if that message is not true it doesn't matter how clearly it's communicated. Someone could give you clear directions that lead you to the wrong destination. The opposite is also true.

Many people wrongly assume that possessing a proper doctrinal stance is all that's important to the faith, but that's like saying breathing is all that's important in life. Is breathing an imperative part of living? Absolutely, but breathing is not where we stop living. It's where life begins. In the same way, doctrine is not the end but the beginning of an effective missional strategy. A Christian can possess a God-honoring theology and simultaneously espouse an ineffective methodology. We must believe the truth, but that truth should naturally lead us to compassionate action. The gospel must be communicated in a loving manner.

Nothing is more tragic than a Christian who spews the truth wrapped in hate. It is unimaginable to consider how some people are able to make the gospel of Jesus Christ look so bad. Like a diamond in the rough, the world often has to break through the outer layer of man-centered religiosity in order to see the beauty of the gospel truth. How should we approach our daily lives as Christ-followers? Listen to these words from Paul found in 2 Corinthians 5:17-20. "Therefore, if anyone is in Christ, he is a new creation. The old has passed away; behold, the new has come. All this is from God, who through Christ reconciled us to himself and gave us the ministry of reconciliation; that is, in Christ God was reconciling the world to himself, not counting their trespasses against them, and entrusting to us the message of reconciliation. Therefore, we are ambassadors for Christ, God making his appeal through us. We implore you on behalf of Christ, be reconciled to God."

We are assigned two major responsibilities in these four short verses. Believers are to represent Christ as Ambassadors, and we are called to become ministers of reconciliation. Notice this all comes as a result of a transformation that takes place in verse 17. This dual calling of ambassador and minister is not a universal description of church members or self-proclaimed Christians. Notice the first few words of the verse. "If anyone is in Christ, he is a new creation." This is a conditional statement only applicable for those who are actually "in Christ."

It's also important to note that the reference to Ambassadors is directly tied to one's having been entrusted with and invested in the message and ministry of reconciliation. In other words we are not truly obedient representatives of Jesus unless we are first reconciling those to Christ who were previously far from the cross. If you're not reconciling people to Jesus, you're not representing Him. No reconciliation – no representation. This is the gospel. Do you want to be like Jesus? Do you want to bring people to Jesus? Then something has got to change.

Christians must stop pushing people away from the cross with prejudice, anger, and ignorance. For far too long believers have allowed their personal preferences, politics, and peripheral doctrines to isolate them from the world Christ called them to save. How we communicate the gospel matters as much as the content of the message we communicates. We must speak truth, but we must do so with His heart. Jesus never condoned sin, but He did reach out to sinners with a loving spirit. If we want to represent Jesus we must show compassion the way He did, refusing to elevate ourselves to the seat of judge. Embrace your calling to reconcile people who are far from Christ. It is not just what we do. This is who we are "in Christ."

CHAPTER EIGHT

PULL BACK THE CURTAIN

I remember the first time I saw *The Wizard of Oz*. It was all so fantastic, with Dorothy, the Tin Woodman, the Lion, and Scarecrow, all determined to make it to the almighty Wizard who had the power to change their unfortunate fate. After working so hard, overcoming unimaginable obstacles, believing all the way that their only hope was in the hands of this great Wizard, this unlikely team discovered a twist in the plot. The Wizard of Oz was no wizard at all. While he had created an illusion that allowed him to appear and sound stronger and more powerful, he was just like the rest of the people, vulnerable and average. Though he was able to fabricate an image of someone or something "great," his tricks couldn't change reality in the long run. Once the curtain was pulled back, the truth was revealed, and the weakness of the Wonderful Wizard was in plain view.

Viewers were very disappointed in the small man who had manipulated the truth and misled Dorothy and her friends. Why would the wizard lie? Why would he attempt to appear to be something he wasn't? This small man was putting on a show to impress others. Perhaps he convinced himself that everyone needed him to be someone better and bigger. Maybe he felt so insufficient that he created this fictitious figure of perfection to offer stability and confidence for those who were searching for a source of hope. And so this man hid his vulnerabilities and eventually believed his own con.

What's Behind Your Curtain?

While no Christian sets out to become a fraud, it's easy to construct a façade and conceal our vulnerability with a figurative curtain that makes us appear stronger, bigger, even better than the rest of the world. While a relationship with Jesus does provide Christians with a unique inner strength to overcome sin's temptation and to endure life's struggles, this strength doesn't provoke the believer to posture himself in a greater position, but a grateful position. Consider these important words from the Apostle Paul in Ephesians 2:8-9. "For by grace you have been saved through faith. And this is not your own doing; it is the gift of God, not a result of works, so that no one may boast."

So salvation has never been and will never be earned by any man or woman, and therefore should not be considered something for anyone to brag about. Sadly, the image projected by most Christians to the world seems to be one of personal pride and self-righteousness. I'm pretty confident that "humility" is not the word your average lost man would use to describe the Christian community. This reminds me of the story found in John 8:1-11 when the Scribes and Pharisees brought an adulterous women to Jesus. They were attempting to trap Jesus in a controversial question surrounding how they should apply the Law of Moses to this situation. Instead of answering them with an extreme response, Jesus simply turned the question on them. "Let him who is without sin among you be the first to throw a stone at her" (John 8:7).

So what's behind your curtain? A sinner is behind our curtain, and we need Jesus. The world doesn't need a fraudulent hope in an earthly wizard. They need Christians to pull back the curtain and give them a Savior. For far too long believers have projected an image that's larger than life, trying to appear to have it all together. Every family dresses up in their finest clothing, polished shoes and perfectly parted hair. They greet one another with the standard, "Good morning! How are you?" The obvious answer is, "Fine, Fine, Fine!" Right? I mean we would never admit we argued all morning, burned a hole in our dress with the iron and spilled our coffee in the car. There's no way any of us would admit we yelled at the kids all the way to church and slammed the car door as we pulled into church. "Fine; Fine; Fine!" Christians have become plastic people who unconsciously project a lie to the world around them.

Perhaps we assumed the world would be attracted to our perceived perfection, but instead we created an unrealistic standard that brought despair to the hearts of those seeking restoration from the brokenness that surrounded them. How could they possibly live up to the standard of the church? They seem to have it all together. Have you seen their Facebook profile at Easter? I mean they have a perfect family! So many outside the church feel completely distant, disconnected, and foreign to the storybook lives of the average Christian. I actually saw a pastor recently make a twitter reference to a pastor wearing a dress shirt while playing softball, and he thought that was a good example to follow for other pastors.

This is exactly the problem. What's behind the curtain? A real person is back there, trying to figure out life himself. Christians are real people who make mistakes. I was born the son of a Southern Baptist pastor, and he served during a generation that expected pastors to live in a fictitious bubble. As his son, I lived inside that bubble where everyone expected us to be perfect. I can remember seeing my dad cut grass in a dress shirt and tie. While my dad's heart was right in doing so, this kind of action created an unnecessary and unhealthy separation between clergy and congregation. It was a different day, and maybe that was the best way to reach people in the 1980s. But it is no longer the 1980s. We've got to pull back the curtain and show the world that we are just as desperate for Jesus as they are.

Why do Christians try to hide their humanity? We are naturally drawn toward a self-dependent religious system. No matter what we know is biblical, most believers slip back into a works mentality, which is unfortunate. Even more basic than that is we just don't want people to see us for who we really are, sinners. And so when they see moral failures from church leaders and church splits on every corner, the world draws some simple conclusions. Those people act like they're perfect and condemn everyone who isn't like them. Followers of Jesus are just real people who are sinners. The only difference in others and us is Jesus.

We keep our fears, discomforts, and doubts behind the curtain. What vulnerabilities could possibly be behind the Christian curtain? Generational tensions, racial division, care for refugees, treatment of women, and the value of life are just a few topics that need to be discussed among conservative Christians. So how do we pull back the curtain? We must open up dialogue on issues that we tend to avoid because they make us uncomfortable. The irony is that we are called to represent Christ as ambassadors, but most of our problems arise because we're representing the concerns of another social or political group. Our faith should drive our decision making process, but I'm afraid many American Christians would agree with that statement, while ignoring the heart of Jesus altogether. Ask yourself this question: Do my actions make me look more like Jesus or the Scribes and Pharisees?

The truth is the curtain isn't really fooling anyone anyway. Sure, people might have believed the Almighty Wizard was real for a while, and there are some people who would believe he existed even after he was exposed, but the show can't go on forever. No one can effectively put on a front that lasts. The projection of the Wizard's image eventually began to fail, and his real identity became undeniably evident to all. We too are vulnerable to the reality of our shortcomings, and our true identities will eventually be revealed even if we refuse to pull back the curtain. We're not perfect, and our lost friends and family know it. We must make an adjustment to our missional strategy. Believers must stop attempting to bring people to Jesus by trying to appear better than everyone else. That is not attractive. In fact, it repels people from Christ.

The world truly is turned upside down, and we know that the only hope is for the body of Christ to turn inside out. The church, however, will never turn inside out as long as we keep playing games, pulling curtains, and projecting false images. The world needs us to start looking and living like Jesus, not hypocritical Pharisees. The only hope for this world is for Christians to get real, be honest about our failures and fear – admit our vulnerabilities and embrace our own need for Jesus. Sure, all Christians verbally confess a personal need for a Savior, but we don't always communicate the same in our daily lives.

Get Real (Be Authentic)

Following Jesus is about BEING not DOING. Jesus spent much of His ministry calling out the counterfeits. The Pharisees were the religious elitists of the day, and they loved to impress others with their personal good deeds of self-righteousness. While their outward actions appeared to be good, their hearts were hard. The Pharisees were the targets of perhaps the most confrontational message Jesus ever preached. Found in Matthew 23:25-28, this sermon was direct and forceful. Jesus didn't dance around the issue and He was not worried about hurting the feelings of these religious leaders. He obviously knew this would be a constant temptation for all religious men. We are all drawn to self-satisfaction and sufficiency in our flesh.

Religion without Jesus ultimately makes us our own god, which is idolatry in the end. Recognizing the sins of the Pharisees and the potential destruction their self-righteous influence would bring, Jesus confronts them head on. Calling them vipers, He called out these religious leaders for their blatant fraudulence. Jesus, in Matthew 23:25-28, accused the Scribes and Pharisees of cleaning the outside, while leaving the inside to rot. "Woe to you, scribes and Pharisees, hypocrites! For you clean the outside of the cup and the plate, but inside they are full of greed and self-indulgence. You blind Pharisee! First clean the inside of the cup and the plate, that the outside also may be clean. "Woe to you, scribes and Pharisees, hypocrites! For you are like whitewashed tombs, which outwardly appear beautiful, but within are full of dead people's bones and all uncleanness. So you also outwardly appear righteous to others, but within you are full of hypocrisy and lawlessness."

Hypocrisy is a spiritual cancer that eats us all alive and ultimately spreads like wicked wildfire. It's so attractive to the human heart that longs for self-sufficiency – longs to be enough. But what can we do? Should we expose the skeletons inside our closets? Obviously, God's will for us all is that we clean out our closets with "clean hands and a pure heart" (Psalm 24:3-4). But what if our tomb is a work in progress? What if we've repented, but God is still working inside us to clean out the undesirable skeletons of sin and shame?

First things first! Stop washing the tombs! In truth, the church is full of sinners. God can use our past failures and even our present imperfections to bring others to faith. Unbelievers need to know that God is calling them to follow Him in obedience, not perfection.

The Decline of Nominal Christianity

How can we pull back the curtain without completely dismantling the mission? In many ways the curtain has already been removed. The world knows that our membership rolls are inflated, and our attendance numbers are waning, and there is a large peripheral segment of the Christian community that is not faithfully following Jesus. Fewer people are claiming to be Christians every year, but many say this does not mean the true church is dying in North American. In fact, many believe this is a good sign in the long run. As the curtain has been removed, many fringe believers have turned away. While it was once considered beneficial, even popular, to be called a Christian, society seems to be trending the other direction in the past few decades. As a result, those with impure motives are falling away. This seemingly unfortunate reality may turn out to be a good grief after all. The true church is shifting from hypocrisy to authenticity.

Researchers have warned us for decades of this coming crisis of Christianity, but the numbers don't tell the whole story. There could be an unseen positive side to this otherwise negative report, the purging of the Body – a spiritual cleansing. As the nominal believers slowly drop off the scene, the true church will remain and actually become stronger in the midst of a numeric decline. It's kind of like a computer that has become bogged down by a myriad of programs running in the background. Restarting the system provides a fresh start and a clean slate.

This restart could provide much benefit to the church in the long run. For example, true believers should become better prepared to face challenges in the days ahead. Cultural conflict will inevitably surround the truth of God's Word, and the church must better prepare the individual believer to defend the faith. Doctrinal awareness is not an optional element of Christianity. True discipleship must be seen as an imperative part of the ministry process. The days of casual Christianity are over, and every believer must commit to grow in his faith. This means we become more intentional about what we teach our children. They should be exposed to the foundational doctrines even in their elementary years. We should continue to equip our kids as they get older, training them in areas previously limited to those in professional ministry. Subjects like apologetics, biblical worldview, and philosophy of religion should be taught to teens prior to going off to college.

We must be a people of strong conviction, who possess a resolve to stay the course, regardless of the personal costs to us. It's not going to be popular to be a Christian in the days ahead. We must prepare our people to live out their faith, not because it's the right thing to do, but because it's who they are in Him. Our confidence in Christ compels us to live out our faith. Christianity is more than a religion observed on Sundays; it is a missional movement that changes lives, communities, and even entire nations. This is a picture of the power of the gospel, and this is what Biblical Christianity looks like.

The Bankruptcy of the Prosperity Gospel

One of the most damaging developments of American Christianity has been the health, wealth, and prosperity gospel, which has spread like cancer fueled by greed and selfish gain. False teachers have knowingly led many people away from the truth into a fabricated Christianity that has money as its mission and "me" as its god. The self-centered theology of the prosperity gospel is disgusting, but people are infatuated by it. Who doesn't want to believe in a religion that is all about their happiness and health? There's one major problem with this theology: it's extra biblical fallacy.

The prosperity gospel has gone bankrupt. No, not financially... they keep raking in the money. Just recently Jesse Duplantis, a Health/Wealth/Prosperity preacher, made headlines for asking his supporters to help him buy a new $54 million dollar jet. His sales pitch for donations was that his current jet requires him to stop too often to refuel.[36] Suffice it to say, people are still fooled by false prophets. Still in the end, the spiritual account is empty, and the followers are no better off than before. The evangelist/pastor may own a new jet or drive a new car, but the followers are spiritually broke. They've ultimately chosen their god: money and possessions. In an effort to find peace of mind and happiness, they sought security in the very thing Christ warned us about.

Jesus knew we'd be drawn toward the worship of materialism and money. So He made His position clear in Matthew 6:24. "No one can serve two masters, for either he will hate the one and love the other, or he will be devoted to the one and despise the other. You cannot serve God and money." Yes, we need to pull back the curtain and expose these impostors who are wolves in sheep's clothing, but we should take a long hard look in the mirror as well. It's easy to point a holy finger at the extreme example of such heresy while displaying symptoms of the same illness. God is not broke, but he doesn't necessarily need his representatives to look like a million dollars (literally).

Some of this flashy materialistic heresy has spilled over into the mainstream church. Many people errantly equate spiritual reverence and holiness with formal clothing. Like it or not this has negatively impacted the expectations of many unbelievers who don't have the money to go shopping for a suit at Macy's. While many argue that we should wear our best when we go to church, this view can and has been taken too far by many. Quite frankly, we can easily make our worship all about us by obsessing over what others are wearing on Sunday morning. Easter Sunday is a good example of this. Everyone comes to worship dressed like they are attending a night at the symphony. We errantly make worship about ourselves in the name of reverence, and we send the message to unbelievers that church is primarily for the wealthy elite.

We must do everything we can to dispel the appearance of a prosperity agenda in the church. The world already sees the church as being a money hungry organization that manipulates people's spiritual vulnerabilities. While generosity is an undeniable characteristic of a mature believer, Christians have not always done a great job of communicating the purpose behind the gift and/or the cause to which the money is being given. We must do everything we can to publically refute the prosperity gospel, while providing consistent evidence of our financial integrity and missional stewardship when spending God's money. Church leaders should have nothing to hide. Pull back the curtain and let the light shine in.

The Race Card

Although not all Christians are racists, Christianity does have a problem with racism. Merriam-Webster Dictionary defines racism as, "a belief that race is the primary determinant of human traits and capacities and that racial differences produce an inherent superiority of a particular race." If you're like the average American, your reaction to a discussion on race either makes you immediately defensive or aggressive toward others. Neither of these responses is productive in the end, and both come from a self-righteous viewpoint.

Our nation is divided on so many fronts, but none more serious than race. This alone is reason for sadness, but worse is the state of the church on the issue. While worship is cultural, and some of our separation is a result of personal preference in church style and methodology, this is only part of the conversation. Unconscious, or at least unacknowledged, discrimination is present in people of every color. It's safe to say that the Christian church remains the most segregated institution in America. We are part of the problem. Allow me to say that this is not a white problem or a black problem. It's not a "you" problem or a "me" problem. This is a sin problem, and the solution will only be found on our knees before God. The time for excuses has passed; people can see through our curtain of spiritual denial.

On one side we see a bunch of white people in denial, oblivious to the ongoing struggle of racial inequality in our day. We must all admit that we struggle at some level. We all become so conditioned to our own unique experience and exposure to society that we neglect to realize that we might be missing something. Just because we don't see it doesn't mean it doesn't exist. So white Americans do have a problem with racism, but then we have another issue few people are willing to discuss, reverse racism. Racism is not a one-way street. People like Al Sharpton and Jesse Jackson, whose coffers grow as racial tensions rise, lead the opposite side of the conversation. They make a living by stimulating feelings of racial victimization blaming white Americans for every injustice imaginable.[37]

So racism and reverse racism are both alive and well in the USA, but shockingly few people want to talk about it. Even when we find someone who admits the presence of racism they tend to point the finger at someone else. CNN writer, John Blake, identifies a new threat, "Racism Without Racists."[38] The truth is we are all drawn to racism in our flesh, because, by definition it puts someone else down and makes much of us. This is a perfect picture of sin's selfish attraction.

Blake writes about a recent racial experiment involving two photographs. The first picture showed an unarmed white man fighting with an armed white man. A second picture displayed an armed white man fighting an unarmed black man. After showing the photographs to the subjects the psychologists asked one simple question related to both pictures. "Which man was armed?" Strangely, the majority identified the armed man correctly in the first photo, but incorrectly in the second. Blake says, "Whites and racial minorities speak a different language when they talk about racism…Some whites confine racism to intentional displays of racial hostility…But for many racial minorities, that type of racism doesn't matter as much anymore…[Common racism] causes unsuspecting people to see the world through a racially biased lens."[39]

Though the vast majority of people consider themselves beyond the evil of discrimination, they get extremely defensive when the discussion makes them feel uncomfortable. So as a result, many simply refuse to discuss the problem, hoping it will magically disappear. This elephant in the room has led us to further cultural compartmentalize the American people, resulting in an undeniable isolationism along the lines of race. Simply bringing up subjects like Affirmative Action, Civil War Monuments, and Immigration Reform, leads people to apply predetermined stereotypes and pass immediate judgment, eventually drawing deep lines in the sand. No one trusts anyone, and as a result the divide widens more every day.

It's obvious that America has a major problem with racism, but no one wants to admit that it's his own. Sure "those people" or that well-known radical group planning marches and demonstrations, they are the racists, right? It's easy to identify the predetermined bias of others. We quickly sense feelings of racial distrust when it's directed toward us, but we're likely blinded to our own prejudiced fears. See, the biggest problem with America's racism is our denial of the problem itself. We're all blind to it, and the ones who feel the least racists may be the guiltiest of all.

Many people have given priority to their politics when dealing with these types of issues, allowing political preferences to drive their spiritual convictions. As a result discrimination has often won over discipleship. Our American rights have somehow trumped our Christian responsibilities. Convictions have become circumstantial, the eventual product rather than the driving factor. Even when people care enough to discuss the hard topics, they're often labeled because of a 20-second sound bite from a 30-minute conversation.

We must begin serious conversations of racial reconciliation, but healing will only come by mutual repentance and Christian love, not fear of loss and endless blame. Virtually every part of our lives has been desegregated, with the exception of one place. Somehow, most churches have maintained their distinct separateness. We can work side by side all week, high five each other at the ball game, and attend the same concerts, but we go our separate ways on Sunday. The one thing that should bring us all together has divided us the most. The church remains the most segregated institution in America.

This is a major problem we all know exists, but no one wants to discuss it. How can people of various races cheer on the same sports team or celebrity, yet not be able to build a bridge of unified worship? While there are many excuses for this disturbing reality, they all remain extra-biblical in nature. It's sad to say that a nightclub on Friday night looks more like heaven ethnically than our churches on Sunday morning. Though Christians should be leading the conversation on race relations, we have isolated ourselves from the world we've been called to reach.

What can we do to help bring racial reconciliation? Sincere acknowledgement of the problem is the first and most difficult step in the process. You can't fix something you're not willing to admit is a problem. I think we all need to remember that the presence of racism doesn't make us racists, but by calling it out in our hearts we're able to overcome it. Another major step towards true reconciliation is to forfeit any claim to provisional repentance. It's so easy to make a conditional agreement rather than an unconditional covenant. There will always be an excuse to hold on to ungodly prejudice, but God is calling us to surrender our excuses.

Once a Christian is personally prepared to begin a conversation on racial reconciliation, he/she should attempt to find small ways to demonstrate a true heart of love to everyone. This will allow your formal commitment to be realized in a more informal setting. Believers need to live it out in daily life. We must also endeavor to create environments for the needed conversations between races. We must be bridge builders who bring people together in the name of Jesus. Debates must be replaced with dialogue as we seek God's heart for every man. Red and yellow, black and white, they are precious in His sight. Pull back the curtain, and let's give them Jesus!

CHAPTER NINE

SURRENDER SELF

Mutual Surrender

No Christian wants to admit he has turned inward because deep down he knows that's not God's will for his life. Jesus summed up the law with two challenges, simple to understand but difficult to fulfill. He commanded us to love God, and love others. "You shall love the Lord your God with all your heart and with all your soul and with all your mind. This is the great and first commandment. And a second is like it: You shall love your neighbor as yourself. On these two commandments depend all the Law and the Prophets" (Matthew 22:37-40). Jesus never commanded us to make ourselves comfortable or to seek our own happiness. No! He called us to surrender.

Still, we fight against this divine call of sacrifice and surrender on our lives, defending our pride and hypocrisy at every step of the journey. We're not chasing after God and His kingdom because we're too busy building our own.[40] Most believers seem more concerned with saving face than serving God. Like a frog in a kettle, American Christians have grown accustom to their confusing surroundings. We've lost sight of the whole reason Jesus came in the first place, the actual purpose of the New Testament church. We have good news to tell - light to shine - life to give; yet we appear to have our heads buried in the sand. What has caused the church to turn inward? Quite simply, a lack of surrender is our issue. Christians need to surrender in many areas, but let's consider two in particular, relationships and leadership.

First, Christians must surrender their **relationships** to God, inside and outside the church. It's easy for Christians to gravitate toward a self-righteous attitude towards unbelievers. While we know that Jesus came to save sinners, we're all just recovering Pharisees, prone to assume the best of ourselves and the worst of others. Sincere surrender requires that we both remember and repent. The worst thing a Christian can do is forget who he was before he met Jesus, but it's equally tragic for that man to remember how much he's been forgiven yet refuse to repent of his judgmental spirit towards others.

We're all desperate for God's grace, but we've learned that it's more difficult to give grace than to receive it. The teachers of the law and Pharisees learned this lesson the hard way in John 8. In the end, they chose to drop the rocks they'd planned on throwing at the adulterous woman, yet many Christians today continue to walk about with pockets filled with self-righteous stones. We must surrender our pride, admitting that we're just real people with serious issues, equally vulnerable to the draw of lust of the eyes and the pride of life. We are just a bunch of unworthy sinners who've been saved by Jesus, and we have come together to lock arms in this God-sized mission to change the world.

Sadly, the low quality of our relationships with unbelievers is only rivaled by our relationships with other Christians. Many churches have a community-wide testimony of being a fighting church, with a heritage of forced church plants that have come as a result of numerous splits over the years. It has to break the heart of God to see His children in constant conflict. Jesus made His expectations clear in John 13:35, "By this all people will know that you are my disciples, if you have love for one another." So, would your community know that your church is a group of His disciples by the way you love each other? What's missing? Mutual surrender is the answer. Christians need to get their eyes back on Jesus and the fields, which are ready for the harvest.

While the unity of the general body of believers is important, the relationship between the pastor and his people is perhaps even more critical. Much of the disunity in the church has come from two unhealthy extremes. Many modern Christians have either become groupies of a celebrity ministry personality, or they have rejected any authority God has placed over them. I'm afraid the mass popularity of a few famous pastoral personalities has led to the deterioration of the reputation and influence of thousands of local pastors across America. While spiritual enthusiasts have continued to follow the spotlight, unbelievers have grown weary of celebrity. As a result, the lost world is searching for something real.

So a pastor should never be worshiped, but faithful church leadership should be followed. We know the culture has been drifting away from all systems of authority for decades, but Christians are in great need of strong, trustworthy **leadership**. Reports of countless moral failures have led to much confusion in the church, but one person's mistake should not lead to our distrust of all people. Just because one leader misled us doesn't mean every leader is corrupt. While we must be wise and discerning, we must also be sensitive to acknowledge when someone possesses strong character.

Still, our trust in leadership should never be blind. I love this balanced explanation from Roy Price. "Trust is a two-way street. Integrity and faithfulness are fundamental to pastor and people alike. Absent in either party, trust languishes. Present- or at least developing-in both, trust flourishes. The benefits are cooperation, peace, and a freedom of relationship that is contagious. Who is responsible to see that trust is developed? The pastor is-if you're a pastor. The layman is-if you're a layman."[41] Yes, Christians should submit to those whom God has placed in positions of authority, but leaders must also surrender themselves to a high level of **accountability** in leadership.

The Surrendered Leader

In order for a leader to surrender he must embrace a **horizontal** style of leadership, a strategic form of leadership that is centered on teamwork at every level. This requires a broadening of the base and a decentralization of the authority. Some church leaders simply can't surrender control, but they ultimately harm themselves and limit their own potential by refusing to invest in others. 21st Century leaders have to make an intentional choice between becoming horizontal leaders and hierarchical dictators. While a clear understanding of authority is imperative in any organization, a great leader can lead without making the followers feel like they're "under" him/her. Instead, they motivate others to follow them on a journey, to accomplish a mission, to believe in a vision worthy of their investment, a cause worth the cost of sacrifice.

Most churches have traditionally embraced a model of positional hierarchy, which tends to focus more on personal power than corporate purpose. I'm not trying to change your church's polity. Instead, the challenge is for us to practically adjust the way we lead. Begin to think horizontal instead of hieratical. When leaders operate in self-centered pride, our personal preferences become the focus and the organization's purpose becomes skewed. Horizontal leadership, on the other hand, is a shared control in which power is dispersed amongst the team and responsibility is distributed equally. There is still a clear line of authority and accountability in cases of incompetence and noncompliance, but everyone is included in the process.

Surrendered leaders learn how to **decentralize** their authority and broaden the base of responsibility. This is important for two reasons. First, no one person should assume the right, nor feel obligated, to carry the entire weight of the leadership responsibility. This is not just applicable to pastoral leadership. Every leader should recognize the need to decentralize their load for the health of the organization. We often unconsciously build organizational systems around ourselves, inadvertently making them dependent on us. Our motivation may be pure, but it's ultimately a selfish move.

"Without counsel plans fail, but with many advisers they succeed" (Proverbs 15:22). When we seek advice from others it provides a newfound leverage of leadership. We're not just leading from our personal decisions, but the collective decisions of many. This provides us with the confidence of confirmation. It's reassuring to hear other competent team members agree with our vision and direction before moving forward. Including other leaders in the decision also produces true buy-in from the team members. The value of this benefit can't be overstated. When our teams are invested in the decision, they will sell it to others. We're not the only one pitching the concept. People don't even have to get their way in order to become a representative of the team's decision. Simply being included in the discussion produces a higher level of confidence in the final outcome.

The second general benefit of broadening the base is a very practical one. The larger the foundation becomes, the higher the building can be constructed. If we build a church on the shoulders of one person, it can only grow so large. I believe most churches reach a growth ceiling that is created by the inability or unwillingness of the senior leaders to share the burden and joy of leadership with others. The church may continue to reach the lost and baptize the saved, but there will be little sustainable growth, because the systems are not built for expansion.

Part of the struggle is that many pastors can't identify people who are willing to step up to the plate and share the load. The pressure most pastors feel is unexplainable, and they are easily misunderstood. Chances are, your pastor needs help, and he may be open to sharing the load of responsibility. Be patient and loving if he needs time to process your offer of help. Pastors often fear the motives of those who want to help, thinking there may be an unspoken agenda. Also be flexible. If our goal is to add value and really bring benefit to our pastor's ministry then we won't be picky when it comes to the area he needs us to serve.

Are you a pastor or senior leader in a church? If you want to grow a church – build a team and invest in them – **empower** them – believe in them. No team will ever rise above your expectations of their ability, and no team will ever rise above our personal example.

Our investment of time, energy, and belief will be the standard by which everyone else is measured. This does not mean we need to sweep floors every week, but it does mean no job is beneath us. Every leader is willing to do whatever it takes because the goal is more important than the role. The corporate cause is worth the individual cost.

Personal pride is the enemy of spiritual surrender, and the only way to overcome it is divine **humility** through God's grace. We need both compelling vision and sincere humility in our leaders. To have one of these without the other is to lead a lonely journey outside the will of God. We must cast a strong vision from a point of meekness. I've heard all my life, "Meekness is not a weakness; it's power under control." The most influential leaders are those who demonstrate a Christ-like spirit of humility. They are strong leaders, but they lead from a place of surrender.

The most successful leaders are those who care more about fulfilling the corporate mission than getting the personal credit. Their strategy is not one of self-promotion but self-sacrifice. The crowds may not be chanting their names, but people will follow them to a faith-filled future. They have learned the secret of self-surrender. "Humble yourself before the Lord, and he will exalt you" (James 4:10). Surrender is ultimately the key to strength.

What is true surrender?

Paul challenges us to defy our pride in Romans 12:3, persuading us to resist the temptation to elevate ourselves above others. "For by the grace given to me I say to everyone among you not to think of himself more highly than he ought to think, but to think with sober judgment, each according to the measure of faith that God has assigned." Everyone wants to talk about the grace we received at salvation, but grace is also continually given by God to believers in order to overcome the temptation of sin. Our flesh will always be drawn to a promotion of self over others, but we must reject it.

The Apostle Paul continues this message in Philippians 2:3-5, "Do nothing from rivalry or conceit, but in humility count others more significant than yourselves. Let each of you look not only to his own interests, but also to the interests of others. Have this mind among yourselves, which is yours in Christ Jesus." Personal pride is at the foundation of all sin, but we see it prevalent inside the church today. I suspect most problems in churches across America are a direct result of Christians seeking their own way. They may veil their religious preference in a fraudulent defense of reverence or a phony pursuit of holiness, but they really just want to have things their way.

So what is surrender and how can it help us turn the church inside out? This process requires submission and humility as believers sacrifice their own agendas in exchange for the plans of God. Personal surrender demands that we are **all-in** when it comes to our missional purpose. There can be no halfway if we're going to attempt to change the world. This is much more difficult than it sounds. After all, everyone claims to be all-in when it comes to God's calling, but most people have a list of missional conditions a mile long. A church turned inside out will be filled with members who are completely committed to the ministry and mission of God, no exceptions.

When we speak of surrender, we're talking about an unconditional covenant, not a circumstantial contract. Someone with a contract mentality is committed as long as everyone else meets his/her expectations. They will do their 50% if the other 50% of the agreement is met. This is why we have Christians who make a lifestyle of church hopping and shopping. Somehow they have embraced a conditional – contractual concept of surrender. The only way we will make a significant impact on this generation is if we get over ourselves and yield everything to Him. God has called us to serve as significant members in a particular local church. He has shaped us like individual puzzle pieces, each with unique design. We're all made with a purpose to be fulfilled among a particular group of believers. We must not miss God's best for us simply because we get our feelings hurt or because something doesn't go our way.

A surrendered believer must be all-in, but he must also be **Christ-centered**. While this is common sense, most Christians seem to miss the obvious. 21st Century Christians have become comfortably numb to the disease of religious consumerism. We've begun to believe this life is all about us, but in truth every Christian's agenda should be purposeful not personal. We must become centered on the gospel, but this will require that everyone give it up. You and I have to surrender our agendas, our preferences, and sometimes even our feelings. Christ should be at the center of every answer, regardless of the question. We must do everything we can to please God, not men.

This ultimately means that everyone has to lay down his/her pride, yielding himself for the glory of God. We don't need a celebrity pastor who thinks he's the next Billy Graham, nor do we need a domineering deacon who thinks he owns the church. Even the sweet little ladies who always think the temperature is too cold and the music is too loud, they must eventually recognize they're not the center of the story. We must all become more Christ-centered if we hope to turn the church inside out. Regardless of our opinions and preferences we must remember, it's not about us at all.

Mutual surrender from all believers will eventually bring collective happiness and missional success to the church. Now this is easier said than done, recognizing the natural tendency of every man to seek after popularity and power. We must acknowledge that this mission is bigger than any one man or woman, and therefore, we must work as a team. We need each other in order to fully embrace the mission and vision God has given to us. Consider the disciples, a very unique group of men from a variety of backgrounds. Jesus didn't call a cookie-cutter group of men to establish and lead the early church. He brought together a diverse group of unique men to accomplish a challenging task. There is strength in diversity, yet few churches are diverse. When the mission is centered on us, we only attract people like us. However, when we center the mission on a compelling vision, we attract a unique group of people based on the vision...not just our personalities.

Better Together

We were made for one another, created to function as a team. Everyone brings a distinctive set of gifts and talents to the table, and that is why we are better together. Believers must acknowledge their own personal weaknesses, which will ironically produce a collective strength among the team. Consider Paul's words in 2 Corinthians 12:10, "When I am weak, then I am strong." We all have weaknesses. Victory comes to those who learn to maximize their strengths while simultaneously depending on the strengths of others. You might coach a baseball team, teach in the local school, serve as a deacon, help in the preschool ministry, or even serve on church staff. No matter what your part, we are better together.

Consider the game of football. Unlike tennis or golf, football is a team sport, and no one player can single-handedly gain the victory. No one can do it all. The running back, quarterback, and the punt returner all need blockers, and a wide receiver can't catch what hasn't been thrown within reach. Some teams may have superstars who possess outstanding specialized skills in one particular area. Others are just superb athletes who rise above the rest, but they are only one of eleven players on the field at any given time. Not only that, they are part of a sub-group of the larger team. The game of football is divided into groups within the team, offense, defense, and special teams. A team could have an excellent defense and lose every game. Winning is truly a team effort. So even the various teams within the team need one another in order to score touchdowns and ultimately win the game, and the best team is a balanced one where every member is both respected and responsible.

Paul addresses this in Romans 12:3-5. "For by the grace given me I say to every one of you: Do not think of yourself more highly than you ought, but rather think of yourself with sober judgment, in accordance with the faith God has distributed to each of you. For just as each of us has one body with many members, and these members do not all have the same function, so in Christ we, though many, form one body, and each member belongs to all the others." This journey is a process of **discovery**, where every individual part makes his/her respective contribution to the betterment of the whole team. God has created us for community, and that community inevitably makes us stronger. We are better together!

What must we change in order to become more surrendered?

Everything has to change. In order for the church to turn inside out and make a significant impact on a world that is turned upside down, we must make some major adjustments. We can reach many people for Christ and never see sustained growth in our churches. Why? We've got to raise the growth ceiling and empower others to help us carry the load. A championship team needs more than good players. Winning also requires a quality coaching staff, but remember that the coach can't get on the field to pass or catch the ball. It's against the rules for him to do it all, yet many church leaders are attempting to do just that. The result is stagnation of the organization and complacency in the team.

Interestingly, when a coach gives 100% to coaching and works to maximize the potential of his team at every level, victory is the result. It's undeniable, great coaching attracts great athletes. Many people see a winning team and assume they could step into the shoes of the coach and win, but in most cases the team's chemistry and success is a direct result of the coach's ability to cast a compelling vision and recruit the right people to accomplish it. Likewise, visionary ministry leaders tend to attract high-level ministry leaders. It's no accident that an awesome team surrounds a "great" pastor. The strong leaders, however, must learn to invest that leadership in others.

What are the benefits of surrender?

Our unreserved surrender will lead the church to naturally turn inside out, allowing it to begin to change a world that's been turned upside down. What are the benefits of this surrender? First, our personal surrender will ensure that God gains the ultimate glory in our lives. He will be in the spotlight, the object of our worship, and the center of our stage. When we make Jesus the target of our glory He will automatically become the author of our story. We are all guilty of wrestling the pen out of God's hand, forcing our own hopes and dreams onto the pages meant for His purpose alone.

We've learned the whole is greater than the sum of its parts. When everyone is given a voice the team's collective song is strong, and the focus becomes less about obeying a man and more about following Jesus. This changes the focus of everything we do. This story is not just personal (Me), nor is it corporate (Us). Our story is divine (His). We are always living in a tension between our individual lives and the greater life of the church God has called us to serve. It is our responsibility to surrender in both settings. We are each his man or woman, but we are one part of His church as well. Surrender takes our personal agendas and makes them purposeful agendas. This means that we begin with what God says not what we say. Scripture has to become the foundation of our ministry and mission. Opinions, traditions, preferences, and policies must all bow their face to the Word of God.

It troubles me greatly to see many Christians elevate their own opinions to the level of scriptural authority. In doing so, they actually lower their view of scripture and jeopardize the legitimacy of their own doctrinal integrity. The practical result of surrendering ourselves to God is a more productive mission and ministry. When everyone on a church staff or ministry team surrenders himself to the greater cause, amazing things begin to happen. There is an immediate increase in individual buy-in. That might seem contradicting on the front in. How can people surrendering their own individual agendas produce an increase in buy-in? It's simple; when everyone demands his/her own way no one ever leaves feeling like they've been heard. A planning meeting filled with unyielding people feels more like a competition for resources than it does a ministry conversation.

So, this mutual surrender produces and elevated morale and involvement from everyone in the faith community. We eventually become more efficient in our efforts, sharing a common cause and intentionally recognizing the value of the whole as being worthy of the sacrifice of its parts. This brings an end to competing systems, turning personal opponents into corporate partners. The world will be impacted, as the church turns inside out for the glory of God. Give up and surrender today.

CHAPTER TEN

AWAKEN TO PURPOSE

Check your vital signs.

There are basically two kinds of Christians in America, those who are asleep and those who are awake. This has obviously been the case for centuries. Paul challenges the early Christians at Rome to wake up in Romans 13:11. "The hour has come for you to wake from sleep. For salvation is nearer to us now than when we first believed." While the current state of slumber among the Christian community is not surprising, it is a crisis that demands our attention.

We often use even more extreme words to describe these two major categories, dead or alive. It's important to make clear that the church of Jesus Christ is marked by life. It has been built on the Rock of Jesus, not on top of a spiritual graveyard. Jesus Himself declared, "The gates of hell shall not prevail against [the church]," Matthew 16:18. God has called all Christians to die to self, but He has also given us new life in Christ. The body of Christ is unmistakably alive, but what do we mean by life?

The word "life" is defined as an organism that possesses "the capacity for growth, reproduction, functional activity, and continual change."[42] Therefore, normal healthy life is characterized by the ability to grow, multiply, and change. Let's apply that definition to our faith. Are most Christians actually growing in their faith? Do most believers multiply themselves by discipling others? Are

Christians normally open to change? By definition, it's safe to say that most Christians are not displaying signs of life. The tragedy is that dead Christians produce dead churches.

Stetzer says that, "Multiplication is a sign of health. Healthy churches multiply disciples, groups, ministries, and churches-- and healthy partnerships cultivate for multiplication among their churches. They plan, structure, and organize for multiplication as a priority. The reality is that healthy living things multiply for the survival of their species. The lack of multiplication is an indicator of an unhealthy organism."[43] This does not mean you're in a "bad" church if this describes you. A corporate church is only as strong as it's individual members. Do you want your church to come back to life? It's time for us to take a hard look at ourselves.

I've heard people throw around the term "dead church" all my life. Admittedly, the worship services at many churches feel more like funerals than celebrations, with dragging music or boring preaching. This has led many believers to declare such congregations dead. This perception, however, is constructed on the misunderstanding that a congregation's lack of inspiration and enthusiasm renders it void of life. Surely a church with a deficient music ministry can still experience true life in Christ. The measurement of life in a church is not based on emotion or experience, but on the willingness of the people to fulfill its mission.

Think back to the definition of *life*, and consider the average Christian in America. If life is the capacity for growth and reproduction, then how can believers who refuse to make disciples claim to be alive? The New Testament church is marked by consistent conversions, ongoing discipleship, church planting, and a willingness to embrace change. These are the signs of life. Do these characteristics describe your church? If not, it is DEAD. When a church is alive it makes an impact on its community. We tend to oversimplify the process and assume that success will ultimately rest on the methodological quality of our product. While these factors are important, they are all secondary to our obedience to the calling of Christ.

First Things First

While this is a multi-faceted issue, spiritual death ultimately comes when we become more concerned about serving ourselves than others. It always comes back to surrender. We may notice some signs of declining spiritual health along the way. We should be concerned when we begin to care more about maintaining than multiplying – when we become more focused on today than tomorrow, and when we care more about rights of ownership than personal investment. Maybe you're not dead yet, but you'd admit you're in the spiritual ICU. Awaken to the mission, and live.

At the core this is a personal problem, a departure from the basic foundations of the Great Commission. We need a grace awakening in America. This will only come when we minimize ourselves and maximize the gospel. This awakening could come if we would only get things in proper priority, first things first. It's all got to start with the message of the gospel. The good news is our primary concern, over respective opinions, circumstantial challenges, and personal preferences. The gospel must become preeminent above all other matters in life, but the gospel is not simply information to internalize. This message must be mobilized!

Our mission flows from the message, but a dead man can't move. This is the problem with many Christians today. They may believe the right information, but they haven't awakened to the message enough to be moved to action. Many people attempt to start with the mission, but this is foolish. Our mission is incomplete without a proper passion for the gospel. Once we've embraced the power and preeminence of the message, however, the mission becomes our primary purpose in life. An awakening to the message and mission comes with an awakening to the Spirit. The Day of Pentecost, recorded in Acts 2, is a good example of how our missional success comes hand in hand with spiritual awakening. We've been sleeping far too long. Wake up Christian! The world is turned upside down, but we can bring hope to this crazy world. May we get up and turn the church inside out for the glory of God.

Focus on the cause.

From the small church across the street to our massive denominational conventions, most people no longer follow the leader just because he has a title or holds a position of authority. Our individual lives should be cause-centric, refusing to cater the mission to our own preferences and opinions. When everyone expects to get his own way on every issue, no one is ever happy. We've got to remember that our entire faith is built upon a sacrifice. God the Son left the perfection of heaven to become a man who willingly died a brutal death, but somehow we think our call to follow Christ is going to be a comfortable journey? Jesus' death was not just a sacrifice to pay our sin debt (justification); it was also a demonstration of how we too must live crucified lives (sanctification).[44] We must remember that we have a cause that is much greater then the cost. Our personal investments will prove to be worth the kingdom return.

As for the church, anyone who hopes to lead a group of believers to an intended destination had better connect their effort to a cause greater than the institution. Leaders must give their followers something to believe in, a purpose worth living for and giving to. The conversation has been changed, and success has been redefined. Where people might have believed in a program in years past, they need a purpose today. The good news is we have one. Our awakening as individual Christians and the awakening of our local churches are both dependent on our embrace of the cause of Christ. His cause is greater than any company, institution, denomination, or leader. This is the mission to which we've been called, and it's a cause worth our sacrifice. I fear we've grown so accustom to sleeping, drawn in by the beauty of our own dreams, that we've forgotten what it feels like to be awakened by the Spirit of God. If we want to invest in something real, we're going to have to wake up and get to work.

While it's important that we possess a cause, it's equally important that we determine a clear direction. I've heard it said, "If you aim at nothing, you'll hit it every time." Biblical community thrives when Christians in that community possesses a common cause, but this cause must be defined. There are endless "good things" to do for the glory of God. One might have a heart for the fatherless, while another faithfully serves the homeless. Others might feel led to minister to a remote tribe in South America, while another coaches a rec team after school. While all of these are legitimate ministries, no one Christian or church can solve every problem.

The frustration we experience in our Christian walk stems from a random approach to purpose. We often say yes to everything that sounds good in the moment and quickly become overwhelmed by the enormity of the collective task. As believers, we must begin to take a more intentional approach to ministry, evaluating opportunities and prayerfully determining which ones best fit the mission to which God has called us. Otherwise, we find ourselves over obligated and burned out in the short-term, when God has called us to a journey.

We should create a standard that helps us determine specific areas that we desire to invest the most of our missional devotion. These items get the most attention and receive the highest priority of our personal resources. Still, there are other opportunities that can and should be on our mission's radar, but we cannot make every good thing a top priority. This brings back to mind our need for a self-discovery to identify gifts and passions that personally drive us. God made us who we are with our personal purpose in mind. Therefore, discovering these things will inevitably help us determine which areas of ministry should receive our greatest amount of time and resources. It's all about becoming better stewards, not just of our money and time, but our lives. How do we start that process? We must begin by asking ourselves these four questions, Why, Where, Who and How.

Self-Evaluation

Question One: Why. Remember, we live in a world turned upside down, but most believers have turned inward and fallen asleep on the job. God is calling us to awaken to a purposeful mission, to move from personal maintenance to purposeful mission. What is it that makes us unique from other people? How can we best prepare ourselves for maximum impact on our mission field? Let's walk through these questions and see how they apply to our lives, ministries, and churches. Let's start with why.

The first step toward our spiritual awakening is for us to clarify our God-given purpose. Why am I doing what I'm doing? What's the point? It's easy for believers to slip into a routine of monotonous activity that makes us feel comfortable, but activity alone doesn't equal purpose. I can run on a treadmill for hours and go nowhere. Like a mouse on a wheel, many Christians are going through the motions, waving at the world outside our cages. We feel a sense of satisfaction and fulfillment because we stay busy at our work, but is it God's work? Are we making a significant impact on this culture? Why are we doing what we're doing?

We've got to stop trying to save the railroad. Simon Sinek, in his book *Start with Why?*, reminds us of an important stage in the history of transportation. The railroad was at one time the major means of transportation and delivery of goods. The executives felt invincible and were determined to maintain the top spot in the field. However, progress, innovation, and advancement in technology proved to be the enemy of the status quo. Sinek makes a remarkable observation related to the strategy driving the vision for the railroad. History records a slow but predictable death for this once superpower.[45] What caused this tragic end?

In the end, the railroad stopped asking "Why?" and went into survival mode. They started out as the leader in transportation, but eventually innovation was replaced by preservation. The executives were more interested in surviving than thriving. As a result the goal became the salvation of the railroad instead of advancement in transportation.[46] It's so easy to become hypnotized by the routine process, invest everything we have in one step on a staircase of a ten-story building. No one step is the end goal of our mission, Instead, each step is a secondary means by which we move closer to the intended primary destination.

Which will gain our greatest allegiance, a program or the purpose? I'm afraid most Christians are living in preservation mode, successfully surviving but not thriving in our missional purpose. Many of us are busy trying to save the railroad, while the world is flying Delta. We're still selling 8-tracks, but the world is listening on Spotify. Like a Blockbuster video store in a Netflix world, many churches are obsolete in the 21st Century. It's more than generational differences; this is a vision problem. Christians have lost sight of our purpose. Christ has not called us to maintain His church, but to mobilize it. We've not been called to save a program or strategy. Instead, we've been called to transport people from darkness to light, from death to life. So why do I do what I do as a Christian? Could it be that our ministry practices are shaped around our family traditions, or maybe our personal preferences? Regardless of what got us here, now is the time for believers to start with why.

Question Two: Where? The second question is one most Christians never ask themselves, where. Where does God want me to serve? Most of us simply don't think of ourselves as missionaries, which makes us feel like we're in charge of our own lives. We are making the decisions related to where our family lives and what we do with our lives. It's like we forget that we no longer belong to ourselves. Followers of Jesus have been purchased and possessed by His sacrifice on the cross. Christ is now in complete control of our lives and holds the keys to our destiny.

Many believers, however, move their church membership as often as they change the oil in their car. Maybe they don't get their way, or they get their feelings hurt. So they move across town to another church fellowship. This makes it challenging for a Christian to ever truly find a personal ministry identity. These people never completely embrace the corporate calling of the church because they can't surrender their own rights and preferences to the larger body of Christ. A Christian who refuses to truly submit himself will never find a permanent place in the missional body of Christ. Many believers simply can't stop worshiping themselves long enough to find their God-given purpose in the church.

God has given me the privilege of serving as Lead Pastor of three churches, all of which are located in very unique cultural context. These experiences have helped me see how we are all missionaries and are called to our own unique mission field. I've served in a small rural church in South Georgia, a medium-sized church in

Metro Atlanta, and now a large First Baptist Church in the Upstate of South Carolina. Each one of these churches had its own unique mission field, and our mission strategy was different for each. While metric reports and methods varied from church to church, the importance of the mission was equal in all three.

At every transition, I was required to learn the people, and to become a student of that unique community culture. This is what God calls every Christian to do. We are not called to go to church; we are commissioned to be the church in the culture where we live. We are to be the light in the darkness. Every Christian reading this book is part of a church with its own unique church culture inside, and it is located in a community that had its own culture outside. "Where" has to be considered by every Christ follower at every turn.

You may be a public school teacher in inner city New York, a fireman in rural Arkansas, or an Executive of a Fortune 500 company. Regardless of your profession, God has called you to be a missionary in the marketplace. Your confession of faith supersedes your professional career. God has called you to serve Him in that community, and He has granted you favor and influence with those people. The context of your mission field, however, is going to be much different from mine. Many have made the mistake of attempting duplicate the success of others by copying everything they do. Many assume this is a short cut to success, but it robs people of their individual cultural identity. Every Christian, every church must consider where God has called them and intentionally consider how they might best make a kingdom impact in that community.

Question Three: Who? Once you have answered the "Why" and "Where" you can move toward answering the "Who." Who has God made you to be? We've determined that you are a missionary, and this is your greatest purpose for living. You have a divine calling to make disciples of Jesus Christ, and He has planted you in a particular mission field. The "Who" may seem complicated on the surface, but it should be an answer that comes most naturally. Complications arise when we feel obligated to be someone we're not, attempting to fit into the cookie cutter mold of the "average believer." In doing so, we neutralize our potential for kingdom impact and lose our greatest benefit, diversity. While Christian unity is essential to missional success, uniformity is the enemy of our God-given purpose. No one will successfully turn the church inside out as long as we are attempting to live up to the latest legalistic expectation of the "experts."

No matter what our profession or passion, God wants to use us for His glory. In order for that to happen, we must endeavor to become the best "us" that we can be. Stop trying to live up to the assumed standard of everyone else. They are not God, and they are not the judges of our faithfulness. The expectations of others are insignificant if they're not based on the Scriptures. God has an unimaginable purpose for every Christian to fulfill, but it's a personal calling. Embrace it! Every Christian has a unique set of skills, gifts, and resources. God had a specific "Who" in mind when He made you and me. It's now our personal responsibility to discover, develop, and deploy these gifts that make us special.

Question Four: How? The average person begins with this question. How can I serve God more faithfully? How can I grow spiritually? How can I make a greater impact on my world? While all these questions are valid, they are secondary steps in the process. We can't effectively answer how until we've dealt with Why, Where, and Who. By nature most of us think we can solve all our problems by changing the methods, but methods are symptoms that flow from identity, and this is why this is where we end, not begin the process. We often think that book all our friends are reading, or a new program we heard about at a conference, is going to save the day. This is a result of improper perspective. We've got to change the way we're looking at our mission.

Our mission is not just methodological; it's organic. This is why our spiritual life is such an important part of the missional equation. The process can never supersede the purpose. While we know it's deeper than methods, we are easily distracted by the promise of a quick fix or a busy project or program that brings a momentary sense of accomplishment and purpose. Our spiritual awakening will not come as a result of changing the things we do. We must start with the heart! While the things we do are very important, they are neither the starting point nor the end goal of our mission.

Methods of our ministry are merely a means by which we fulfill our God-given purpose. So how do we set out to answer the "How?"

Missional Adaptation

After evaluation comes adaptation. Believers must adjust at every stage of life. We understand this in other areas of our lives, but we often forget to make the needed changes in our faith walk as our life circumstances change. We get stuck as a result of this unconscious neglect. From personal walk to congregational methodology, to denominational vision, we must embrace change. We've all heard it said many different ways. Methods are always changing, but the message of the gospel must remain the same. Still many Christians refuse to change their personal approach to life and living, remaining stuck in the methodological rut of their past. I recently read that Netflix founder, Reed Hastings, offered to sell his company to Blockbuster CEO, John Antioco for $50 million back in 2000. Antioco's decision to pass on this offer goes down as one of the most foolish business decisions in history as Netflix value has now hit an all-time high of $56 billion.[47]

I'm sure you know the story of Blockbuster's eventual death, and the inevitable rise of new technologies. Those who adapted to these changes continued to find success. Others, like Blockbuster, assumed they were above the fray, exempt from vulnerability and failure. We've got a lot of Blockbuster Christians in a Netflix world. This applies to everything from our personal routines and our parenting strategies. Even our interactions and the relevance of our leadership in our local church are drastically impacted by our willingness to adjust as the culture changes. We can attempt to deliver the gospel via videotape like Blockbuster, but that system of delivery is no longer effective today. We've spent a lot of time blaming the next generation for rejecting a Blockbuster gospel. Stop blaming, and start claiming them!

The Christian life is filled with change and challenge. We are constantly required to adjust in order to advance, but we are never permanently finished making adjustments. Change is an inevitable part of our identity. We must all make personal adjustments on a regular basis if we desire to make a significant impact in the next generation. If we're selling 8-tracks in the 21st Century...no one will hear our song. A Christian or church that refuses to change its approach is bound for eventual death. While we never compromise truth in the process, we choose life as we advance the gospel to our children and grandchildren.

Missional Execution.

Sadly, we could make every preparation necessary to discover our pathway to spiritual awakening and willingly adapt to the many cultural changes around us, and still refuse to deploy the plan we've discovered. We must do more than complain about the moral decline in our day. Christians must move beyond the rubberneck tendencies of a passing motorist, watching as the bodies are pulled from the damaged cars. We are the ones made for rescue. Wake up! Let's commit together to do more than talk about it. We must take steps today to begin the intentional process of turning our lives inside out. Then we can promote this awakening to our local churches, as the Holy Spirit leads other Christians to awaken to His purpose for their lives.

So what's the next step? I hope and pray God has convicted your heart to drop the rocks, put on the boots, pull back the curtain, and become the missionary God has created you to be. We've got to stop wasting time on needless arguments and distractions, and get back to our kingdom mission. You are a leader with a specific sphere of influence, and you can make an impact in this generation for the glory of God. Don't waste your life on you or anyone else! This world is turned upside down, but hope remains in Jesus Christ. How will they hear of this Savior and the hope of forgiveness and eternity we have found in Him? The only hope for a church turned upside down is a church turned inside out. What is the answer? You are it!

FINAL CHALLENGE

Where do we start?

Living out our Christian faith in the 21st Century can be an overwhelming endeavor. Surrounded by the chaos and confusion of the culture, we might easily assume that believing the truth is all that matters. The manner in which we share the gospel, however, is just as important as the message itself. Nothing is more tragic than a Christian who spews the truth wrapped in hate. It's unimaginable to consider how some people manage to make the good news look so bad. Like a diamond in the rough, the world often has to break through the outer layer of man-centered religiosity in order to see the beauty of the gospel truth. How should we approach this Inside Out challenge? Listen to these words from Paul one more time.

"Therefore, if anyone is in Christ, he is a new creation. The old has passed away; behold, the new has come. All this is from God, who through Christ reconciled us to himself and gave us the ministry of reconciliation; that is, in Christ God was reconciling the world to himself, not counting their trespasses against them, and entrusting to us the message of reconciliation. Therefore, we are ambassadors for Christ, God making his appeal through us. We implore you on behalf of Christ, be reconciled to God." 2 Corinthians 5:17-20

Our two major responsibilities are to represent and reconcile. Christ has called us to be Ambassadors, but as we represent Him we must also reconcile others to Him. Don't miss this! Both of these responsibilities come as a result of a transformation that takes place in verse 17. This dual calling of ambassador and minister is not a universal description of church members or self-proclaimed Christians. Notice the first few words of the verse. "If anyone is in Christ, he is a new creation." This is a conditional statement only applicable for those who are actually "in Christ."

It's also important to note that the reference to Ambassadors is directly tied to one's having been entrusted with and invested in the message and ministry of reconciliation. In other words, we are not truly obedient representatives of Jesus unless we are first reconciling those to Christ who were previously far from the cross. If you're not reconciling people to Jesus, you're not representing Him either. No reconciliation – no representation. This is the gospel.

We must stop pushing people away from the cross with prejudice, anger, and ignorance. For far too long believers have allowed our personal preferences, politics, and peripheral doctrines to isolate us from the world Christ came to save. We must speak truth, but we must do so with the heart of Jesus. While He never condoned sin, Jesus did reach out to sinners in love. If we want to represent Him we must show compassion the way He did, refusing to elevate ourselves to the seat of judge. What can we do in this world that's been turned upside down? Join me by embracing our calling to turn the church inside out.

ENDNOTES

1. Dickens, Charlse. A Tale of Two Cities. Black and White Classics: NY. 2014, 3.
2. Groothuis, Douglas. 2000. *Truth Decay: Defending Christianity Against the Challenges of Postmodernism*. Downers Grove, IL: Inter Varsity Press, 212.
3. Groothuis, Douglas. 2000. *Truth Decay: Defending Christianity Against the Challenges of Postmodernism*. Downers Grove, IL: Inter Varsity Press, 55.
4. Thoreau, Henry David. 2015. A Week on the Concord and Marrimack Rivers. Scope Publishing (ebook).
5. Groothuis, Doulas. 2000. *Truth Decay: Defending Christianity Against the Challenges of Postmodernism*. Downers Grove, IL: Inter Varsity Press, 225.
6. Andy Stanely Message (August 20, 2018) www.youtube.com/watch?v=AyvtIX_8BJs
7. Groothuis, Douglas. 2000. *Truth Decay: Defending Christianity Against the Challenges of Postmodernism*. Downers Grove, IL: Inter Varsity Press, 53.
8. Taylor, Paul. 2014. *The Next America*. USA: Public Affairs Books, 3.
9. https://www.yahoo.com/news/will-never-another-billy-graham-world-made-possible-gone-195847056.html
10. Taylor, Paul. 2014. *The Next America*. USA: Public Affairs Books, 11 & 44.
11. www.dictionary.com/browse/utilitarianism
12. Twenge, Jean and W. Keith Campbell. 2009. *The Narcissism Epidemic: Living in the Age of Entitlement*. NY: Atria Paperback,128.
13. Mill, John Stuart. 2017. *Utilitarianism*. Overland Park, KS: DigiReads Publishing,10.

14 https://www.scu.edu/ethics/ethics-resources/ethical-decision-making/calculating-consequences-the-utilitarian-approach/
15 Mill, John Stuart. 2017. *Utilitarianism*. Overland Park, KS: DigiReads Publishing, 40-47.
16 Mill, John Stuart. 2017. *Utilitarianism*. Overland Park, KS: DigiReads Publishing, 25.
17 Twenge, Jean and W. Keith Campbell. 2009. *The Narcissism Epidemic: Living in the Age of Entitlement*. NY: Atria Paperback, 18.
18 Twenge, Jean and W. Keith Campbell. 2009. *The Narcissism Epidemic: Living in the Age of Entitlement*. NY: Atria Paperback, 247-249.
19 Twenge, Jean and W. Keith Campbell. 2009. *The Narcissism Epidemic: Living in the Age of Entitlement*. NY: Atria Paperback, 123.
20 Twenge, Jean and W. Keith Campbell. 2009. *The Narcissism Epidemic: Living in the Age of Entitlement*. NY: Atria Paperback, 162.
21 Groeschel, Craig. 2012. *Soul Detox*. Grand Rapids: Zondervan, 109.
22 www.azquotes.com/quote/1155090
23 https://thewaterproject.org
24 www.desiringgod.org/articles/spiritual-awakening-and-the-knowledge-of-god#awakening
25 Trey Gowdy. Speaking at Second Baptist Houston, Texas. Sunday August 12, 2018.
26 http://www.bpnews.net/50860/evangelicalism-needs-to-focus-on-cross-moore-says
27 http://griddiron.com/blog/2017/6/16/how-to-lead-a-politically-diverse-church
28 http://www.journalism.org/2016/07/07/pathways-to-news/
29 http://smallbusiness.chron.com/generational-marketing-characteristics-74962.html
30 Warren, Rick. 1995. *The Purpose-Driven Church*. Grand Rapids: Zondervan, 168-172.
31 http://chucklawless.com/2018/05/why-some-churches-are-doing-away-with-childrens-church/
32 Smith, Robert. 2008. *Doctrine that Dances: Bringing Doctrinal Preaching and Teaching to Life*. Nashville: B & H Academic, 1.
33 Micah Fries Twitter Post: August 23
34 www.bpnews.net/50952/firstperson-its-not-about-us

35. www.washingtonpost.com/news/politics/wp/2018/05/24/the-group-least-likely-to-think-the-u-s-has-a-responsibility-to-accept-refugees-evangelicals/?utm_term=.25edee4cc2c1
36. www.cbsnews.com/news/jesse-duplantis-evangelist-private-jet-jesus-wouldnt-be-riding-donkey-2018-05-29/
37. http://www.digitaljournal.com/article/254754
38. www.cnn.com/2014/11/26/us/ferguson-racism-or-racial-bias/index.html
39. www.cnn.com/2014/11/26/us/ferguson-racism-or-racial-bias/index.html
40. Matthew 6:33
41. www.christianitytoday.com/pastors/1980/spring/80l2047.html
42. https://en.oxforddictionaries.com/definition/life
43. STETZER, ED. MULTIPLYING IN PARTNERSHIP: THOUGHTS ON THE WORK OF DENOMINATIONS & NETWORKS: HOW CHURCH PARTNERSHIPS CAN HELP FOSTER MULTIPLICATION. CHRISTIANITY TODAY: SEPTEMBER 23, 2013.
44. Galatians 2:20
45. Sinek, Simon. 2009. *Start with Why*. NY: The Penguin Group, 50-51.
46. Sinek, Simon. 2009. *Start with Why*. NY: The Penguin Group, 50-51.
47. www.businessinsider.com/blockbuster-ceo-passed-up-chance-to-buy-netflix-for-50-million-2015-7

Made in the USA
Columbia, SC
02 May 2019